BORN WITH A
CREATIVE TEMPERAMENT

THE SANGUINE-MELANCHOLY (I-C)

John T. Cocoris, PSY.D.

11-16-19

ISBN 978-0-9721650-1-3
Library of Congress Card Number:

Profile Dynamics
McKinney, Texas 75070

Cover and interior design by April Beltran

ACKNOWLEDGMENTS

I am indebted to my wife, Darrellene, who shares my vision for this work. We have spent countless hours talking about observations we have both made. She has read and reread the manuscript making helpful suggestions. I am indebted to my brother, Mike, for his guidance and support. He has made valuable contributions to this work. A special thanks to Gary Fusco who edited the manuscript. He shares my passion for using the temperament concept in counseling. Thanks also to Lane Hedgepeth for reading and editing the manuscript. A special thanks to April Beltran who read and edited the manuscript offering insightful suggestions that has made this work better. April is also responsible for the interior layout and the book cover design.

WHAT YOU'LL DISCOVER INSIDE

Why Do People Do What They Do?   *1*

01   THE TEMPERAMENT CONTEXT   3

02   12 EARLY SIGNS   19

03   SELF-AWARENESS   31

04   THE SANGUINE-MELANCHOLY (I-C) TEMPERAMENT   37

How To Maximize Your Potential   *49*

05   BE WITH PEOPLE   51

06   SPEND TIME ALONE   55

07   OPERATE FROM A PLAN   61

08   DEVELOP COPING SKILLS   65

09   CONTROL YOUR THOUGHTS & EMOTIONS   79

10   CONTROL YOUR MOODS   85

11   DO NOT BE CONCERNED ABOUT YOUR IMAGE   91

12   CONTROL YOUR NEED TO TALK   99

When they focus on goals and use their natural abilities productively, there is almost nothing they cannot accomplish.

13	BE CREATIVE	103
14	BE A GOOD COACH	107
15	USE POSITIVE SELF-TALK & VISUALIZE SUCCESS	111
16	MAKE HEALTHY CHOICES	121
17	HAVE A POSITIVE IMPACT	125
18	GET A GOOD NIGHT'S SLEEP	129

19	SELF-AWARENESS EXERCISE	135
20	THE USE OF MEDICATION	139
21	SUCCESS STORIES	149

Conclusion	*157*
A NOTE FROM THE AUTHOR	159
ABOUT THE AUTHOR	161
APPENDIX	163
HOW TO DEAL WITH FRUSTRATION	165
DEVELOP A PHILOSOPHY OF LIFE	167

"WHY DO PEOPLE DO WHAT THEY DO?"

I began my long journey in 1974 to understand and develop the temperament model of behavior. I did not know what I was looking for, I was just looking. My journey led me into and then out of the ministry. I entered the field of consulting to promote the application of the temperament model of behavior in business. I eventually decided to develop and promote the application of the temperament model of behavior in the field of counseling. That part of the journey led me to get a Master's degree in counseling and then a Doctorate in Psychology. I became a licensed therapist in Texas and established a counseling private practice. That part of the journey led me to work for a time in a mental health hospital in Dallas, Texas.

I mentioned all of this to establish the context in which I made some discoveries about the temperament concept, in particular, the creative temperament. This book is about this creative, yet complex temperament blend.

Have you ever asked, *"Why do people do what they do?"* There are many different ways to answer this question from the field of psychology which officially began in the late 1800's. I investigated the major theories of personality and found them lacking in a satisfactory explanation--at least until I was introduced to the concept of temperament. This concept, I believe, is the best explanation of "Why do people do what they do?" that I have seen.

Hippocrates, the Father of Medicine (c. 460-377 B.C.) is credited with its beginning 2,400 years ago. Actually there is evidence that the ancient Chinese originated the idea hundreds of years before Hippocrates. References are even found in the early writings out of Egypt and Mesopotamia. Others followed Hippocrates adding clarity to his foundation. For a more complete treatment of the subject see my book, *The Temperament Model of Behavior: Understanding Your Natural Tendencies* (2014).

I have investigated and validated people's temperaments by talking one-on-one to thousands of people since I was introduced to the concept. This book represents what I have learned about creative people as a result of my research.

This book is about a person who is born with certain natural tendencies which produces an active and creative mind. Their creativity is usually seen early in their life and includes ability in art, music, writing, design, interior decorating, architecture, cooking, and more. They can excel in writing songs, singing songs, playing any musical instrument (they especially like the guitar), acting, painting works of art, writing poetry, and excelling in sports. Some are just great at problem solving. The person who possesses these natural tendencies is capable of excelling to the top of whatever field they choose. History is filled with the great works of these gifted and talented people.

Their natural tendencies include a need to be with people most of the time and to be alone some of the time. They naturally have difficulty going to sleep and staying asleep. Their mind never stops processing information.

This combination is a unique blend of natural tendencies that no one else possesses, but it is not without internal tension. This person has a natural tug-of-war inside pulling them in two different directions--most often at the same time. One part wants to be with people and the other part wants to be alone to think and plan.

When these natural tendencies are understood and controlled, there is not much this person cannot do as good as, or better than, anyone else. When these natural tendencies are not understood and controlled, this person is often confused and frustrated. Is this you? If so, I have good news! This book will help you understand and control your natural temperament tendencies so that you may maximize your enormous potential.

John T. Cocoris
McKinney, Texas

01

THE TEMPERAMENT CONTEXT

THE TEMPERAMENT CONTEXT

I have written a series of books and manuals on the subject of temperament. Each work represents a different application of the concept. In order to adequately understand each application, it was necessary to include in each work a variation of the history of the temperament concept, foundational concepts, and common questions. If this is the only book you read on the subject of the temperaments you would need the information in the first few chapters. Much of the material found in chapter one is also found in more detail in my book, *The Temperament Model of Behavior: Understanding Your Natural Tendencies.*

The concept of the four temperaments has been around for thousands of years as mentioned. Simply put, people are born with natural tendencies that can be grouped into four categories. The most archaic terms used are Choleric, Sanguine, Phlegmatic and Melancholy. The most popular terms used today are High D (Dominant), High I (Influencing), High S (Steadiness), and High C (Compliance). The correlations of the terms are Choleric (D), Sanguine (I), Phlegmatic (S), and Melancholy (C).

According to the temperament model of behavior, every person has all four tendencies to some degree, but one of the four has a greater influence than the other three. The primary tendency has the main influence on a person's behavior while another tendency has a secondary influence and so forth. It is the combination of the top two tendencies which produce a blend that urges a person to consistently behave in a particular manner.

In the last half of the twentieth century there has been a revival of interest in the four temperament concept in the United States. Almost all of the material written has a focus only on a person's primary temperament. The focus in this concept is not just the primary temperament but the combination of the two strongest tendencies. Considering the temperament *blend* of a person versus only thinking in terms of the primary temperament is like putting a fuzzy picture in focus. In dealing with the temperament concept, it is essential to deal with the blend of the first two temperaments.

The overview chart (see Figure 1) shows various names used to refer to the temperaments. Many more have been used but these seem to be the most popular ones. The chart also shows the kind of outlook each temperament has on life.

PRIMARY TEMPERAMENT SUMMARY CHART
FIGURE 1

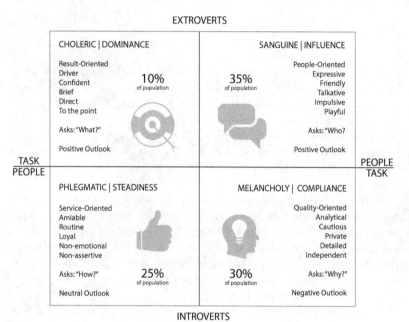

EXTROVERTS

CHOLERIC | DOMINANCE

Result-Oriented
Driver
Confident   10%
Brief   of population
Direct
To the point

Asks: "What?"

Positive Outlook

SANGUINE | INFLUENCE

People-Oriented
Expressive
35%   Friendly
of population   Talkative
Impulsive
Playful

Asks: "Who?

Positive Outlook

TASK
PEOPLE

PEOPLE
TASK

PHLEGMATIC | STEADINESS

Service-Oriented
Amiable
Routine
Loyal
Non-emotional
Non-assertive

Asks: "How?"   25%
of population

Neutral Outlook

MELANCHOLY | COMPLIANCE

Quality-Oriented
Analytical
Cautious
Private
Detailed
Independent

30%   Asks: "Why?"
of population

Negative Outlook

INTROVERTS

HISTORICAL OVERVIEW

HIPPOCRATES (C. 460-377 B.C.)

Hippocrates is given credit for observing that people have natural tendencies (temperament). He taught that behavior was determined by the presence of an excessive amount of one of four fluids or humors: yellow bile (Chlor), red bile or blood (Sangis), white bile (Phlegm) or black bile (Melan). By isolating these four fluids he was trying to establish that behavior has a medical origin.

GALEN (AD 129-200 OR 216)

Galen was a Greek physician who lived 600 years after Hippocrates. He related the four temperaments to illness. He is credited with coining the terms Choleric,

Sanguine, Phlegmatic, and Melancholy in his dissertation *De temperamentis*.

NICHOLAS CULPEPER (1616-1654)

Nicholas Culpeper was an English botanist, herbalist, physician, and astrologer. He rejected the idea that the four humors were the cause of a person's temperament. He also was the first to say that a person is influenced by two temperaments, one primary and one secondary. Before Culpeper, it was believed that a person was influenced by only one temperament.

IMMANUEL KANT (1724-1804)

Immanuel Kant, a German philosopher, described the temperaments in his book, *Anthropology from a Pragmatic Point of View* (1798). He wrote a description of the four temperaments that was clear and accurate.

CARL JUNG (1875-1961)

Carl Jung, a Swiss psychiatrist, published *Psychological Types* in 1921. The premise of his work was to determine how people take in information and make decisions. Jung coined the terms extrovert and introvert suggesting that everyone falls into one of the two categories. The extrovert prefers the outer, objective world of things, people and actions; and the introvert prefers the inner, subjective world of thoughts, ideas, and emotions.

WILLIAM M. MARSTON (1893-1947)

William M. Marston was the first to contribute scientific evidence that people fit into one of four categories. He published his book, *Emotions of Normal People* in 1928 using the terms Dominant, Influence, Steadiness and Compliance.

OLE HALLESBY (1879-1961)

Ole Hallesby, a Lutheran theology professor in Norway, contributed penetrating insight into temperament behavior. In his book *Temperament and the Christian Faith*, written in the 1930's, he used the terms Choleric, Sanguine, Phlegmatic, and Melancholy.

ISABEL MYERS (1897-1980) AND KATHARINE BRIGGS (1875-1968)

Isabel Myers and her mother, Katheryn Briggs, wrote a paper in 1958 titled Myers-Briggs Type Indicator (MBTI) in which they proposed that there are sixteen different personality types. Their work was based on Carl Jung's writings on psychological types.

TIM LAHAYE (1926-   )

Tim LaHaye was the first to popularize the temperament concept within the Christian community. Dr. LaHaye published the first of several books in the 1960's using the terms Choleric, Sanguine, Phlegmatic, and Melancholy. He was the first to write in detail about the dynamics of the temperament blends.

JOHN G. GEIER (1934-2009)

John G. Geier built on the previous works of William M. Marston (1928), Walter Clarke (1940) and John Cleaver (1950). John Geier coined the terms High D (Dominant), High I (Influencing), High S (Steadiness), and High C (Competent).

OTHERS

Others have contributed to the temperament model of behavior; Plato (350 BC), Paracelsus (1530), Adickes (1905), Spranger (1914), Kretschmer (1930), Adler (1937), Fromm (1947), Eysenck (1951), and Keirsey (1970).

FUNDAMENTAL CONCEPTS

The temperament model of behavior is based on several foundational concepts. Understanding these concepts is essential to correctly applying the temperament model to behavior.

EACH PERSON HAS A BLEND OF A PRIMARY AND SECONDARY TEMPERAMENT

Everyone has traits of all four temperaments but all four are not present with equal influence on behavior. The primary temperament will have a stronger influence on behavior than the other three. Of the remaining three, the secondary temperament will have a stronger influence on behavior than the remaining two. The second temperament will always modify the tendencies of the primary temperament in some significant way. The blend of the primary and secondary temperaments will represent a person's normal, usual, and daily demeanor.

EACH TEMPERAMENT HAS NATURAL STRENGTHS AND WEAKNESSES

Each person will naturally excel at certain tasks while being naturally deficient in performing other tasks. For example, the Sanguine works well with people but is usually weak when working with details, whereas the Melancholy works well with details but will shy away from too much involvement with people.

STRENGTHS AND WEAKNESSES REPRESENT BOTH TEMPERAMENTS

All twelve blends will combine strengths and weaknesses representing both temperaments. For example, the Choleric-Melancholy (D/C) will combine the strengths and weaknesses of both the Choleric (D) and the Melancholy (C). This produces a person who gets results with a detailed plan and can be forceful, explosive, and critical, but can also be gentle and sensitive.

STRENGTHS AND WEAKNESSES VARY IN DEGREES OF INTENSITY

The intensity of traits present have significant influence on the expression of a person's temperament tendencies. Two people with the same temperament may demonstrate differences in behavior because one is more intense than the other. Intensity levels vary from mild, to moderate, to extreme.

A STRENGTH OVEREXTENDED BECOMES A WEAKNESS

Any strength that is overextended (used to an extreme) will become a weakness. For example, the Choleric (D) is naturally brief, direct, and to the point in their communication with others but if they are too direct they become blunt and offensive. The Sanguine (I) tends to talk a lot but if they talk too much they will annoy others. The Phlegmatic (S) is naturally accommodating but if they are too accommodating others will take advantage of them. The Melancholy (C) is naturally analytical but if they are too analytical they will be paralyzed and never get anything done.

STRENGTHS CAN BE DEVELOPED AND WEAKNESSES CAN BE OVERCOME

Each person has the choice to develop their natural temperament strengths and overcome their natural temperament weaknesses. Whether or not a strength is developed or a weakness is overcome and to what degree depends on the individual's motivation to become a more well-balanced person.

TEMPERAMENT TENDENCIES ARE DEVELOPED ACCORDING TO A PERSON'S RESPONSE TO THE VARIABLES IN THEIR ENVIRONMENT

Differences in behavior may be explained by an individual's response to the many variables to which a person is exposed to in their environment. Environment does not determine temperament, but it can influence development by accentuating strengths or weaknesses. A person is always responsible for the choices they make regardless of their environment.

TEMPERAMENT IS AN INNER FORCE THAT PUSHES AND PULLS

This principle enables us to understand the dynamics that occur when the various temperaments are combined. All temperament blend combinations experience internal conflict on some level. The nature of the conflict is that two temperaments representing two different and sometimes opposing forces are at work at the same time pushing and pulling the person in two different directions. One temperament will push on the individual to act, and at the same time, the other will pull the individual back from acting which produces internal tension.

For most of the blends the internal conflict or tension is not a major issue. There are a few of the blends, however, where the push/pull causes a more serious level of internal conflict and tension. For example: the combination of Choleric (D) and Melancholy (C) produces some tension because there is an urgent need to get results conflicting with the need to get right results; the combination of Sanguine (I) and Melancholy (C) produces tension because there is a need to be with people conflicting with the need to be alone; and the combination of Melancholy (C) and Choleric (D) produces tension because there is need to get right results and the Melancholy (C) will resist being pushed to get results quickly.

FREQUENTLY ASKED QUESTIONS

WHAT IS TEMPERAMENT?

Temperament represents the way a person relates to others and responds to events. It is what you have observed and expect someone's behavior to be, most of the time. Have you ever referred to someone as shy or outgoing? Without realizing it, you were referring to certain temperament traits. These traits are what you know and expect the person to be every time you are with them.

The four temperaments are represented by four distinct groups of traits or tendencies. Each cluster of traits produces a distinct manner of behavior that is different from the other groups. For example, the Choleric is result-oriented, the Sanguine is people-oriented, the Phlegmatic is service-oriented, and the Melancholy is quality-oriented. Thus, temperament behavior is, for the most part, predictable. The exception being when one temporarily experiences strong emotions, such as anger or fear, or is trying to deceive another. Actually, acting is a form of acceptable deception. A person is knowingly acting like they are someone else. Unfortunately, some purposely act like someone they are not in order to deceive.

Because someone's temperament is inborn, it is a force which pushes or urges you to behave according to the tendencies that represent your temperament blend. You can also think of temperament as a need. Abraham Maslow says that a need is something that if you do not meet, you become sick. Air, food, and water are physical needs without which a person would become ill and die. If your temperament needs are not met, you will not die but you will become emotionally and eventually physically ill. Stress-related illness is often the result of a temperament need not being met. Meeting temperament needs is critical to a person's sense of well-being and feeling of self-worth.

WHAT A TEMPERAMENT IS NOT

Many people often confuse temperament with character, personality or type. First of all, temperament has nothing to do with a person's character or their level of maturity. Character reflects the choices that are made. A person's temperament is also not the same as their personality. There are many factors that make up the total personality of a person—temperament is only one part. Lastly, temperament is not a type. Types are broad categories such as extrovert or introvert. Someone's temperament, as mentioned in the section above, is composed of traits. While types are broad categories, traits are more narrow and specific characteristics of behavior such as being direct, sociable, patient, or analytical.

NOTE: The temperament model does not embrace the type approach to behavior. Rather, the temperament model recognizes that people are born with a cluster of traits which allows for different degrees of expression or development by an individual. Gordon Allport says, "A man can be said to have a trait; but he cannot be said to have a type, rather he fits a type."

WHAT IS THE ORIGIN OF TEMPERAMENT?

There are two possibilities: either people are born without natural tendencies, or they are born with natural tendencies. Some believe that people start life as a blank slate (referred to as tabula rasa) and that the environment determines the personality as individuals have exchanges with their environment. Others teach that a person is born with natural tendencies and that these traits are developed according to that person's response to their environment.

The temperament model of behavior teaches that people are born with traits. If you want proof that children are born with natural tendencies just ask a mother who has raised at least two children. She will tell you that they were different from birth. My daughter has twin girls and knew before they were born that one was going to be very active and the other one was going to be more gentle and that is exactly how they are today.

WILL MY TEMPERAMENT BLEND EVER CHANGE?

No. The temperament blend that you were born with remains throughout your life-span. Some think that because they have experienced some growth their temperament blend has somehow changed. All that has really happened is that they have learned self-control and have matured.

CAN ANYONE BE A LEADER OR MANAGER REGARDLESS OF THEIR TEMPERAMENT?

Yes. Each person will lead differently according to their temperament blend. The Choleric and Sanguine will lead by directing. They will tell you to get a task completed. The Phlegmatic and Melancholy will lead by example. They will show you how to complete the task. Each one will be effective in their own way.

THE FOUR PRIMARY TEMPERAMENTS

As has been pointed out, there are four primary temperaments. The first two are extroverts and the other two are introverts. Extroverts are active and process oriented. From their point of view, the environment is made to provide the satisfaction that they want. Introverts tend to be passive, private, and accommodating. They tend to adapt to whatever the environment has to offer. They are production oriented. Here is a brief explanation of the four primary temperaments:

CHOLERIC | The Choleric is extroverted, hot-tempered, quick thinking, active, practical, strong-willed, easily annoyed, and result-oriented. The Choleric has a huge ego, a firm expression, and is self-confident, self-sufficient, and very independent minded. They are decisive, opinionated and find it easy to make decisions for themselves as well as others.

SANGUINE | The Sanguine is extroverted, impulsive, fun-loving, activity-prone, entertaining, persuasive, easily amused, optimistic, and people-oriented. The Sanguine tends to be competitive, impulsive, and disorganized. The voice of the Sanguine will show excitement and friendliness. They have a natural smile and talk easily and often. They are animated, excitable, and accepting of others. They build relationships quickly and have lots of friends.

PHLEGMATIC | The Phlegmatic is introverted, calm, unemotional, slow moving, easygoing, accommodating, and service-oriented. The Phlegmatic does not show much emotion and will have a stoic expression. They are slow to warm up and indirect when interacting with others. The Phlegmatic lives a quiet, peaceful, routine life, free of the normal anxieties of the other temperaments. They avoid getting too involved with people and life.

MELANCHOLY | The Melancholy is introverted, logical, analytical, factual, private, conscientious, timid, and quality-oriented. The Melancholy will (most always) have a serious expression. They usually respond to others in a slow, cautious, and indirect manner. They are self-sacrificing, creative, and can be perfectionists. The Melancholy has high standards to avoid mistakes.

THE TWELVE TEMPERAMENT BLENDS

This will be a brief overview of the twelve blends. Blends with the same primary temperament will have many tendencies in common as well as many tendencies that differ due to the influence of the second temperament. For a more in-depth treatment see, *The Temperament Model of Behavior: Born With Natural Tendencies*, by John T. Cocoris.

 ### THREE CHOLERIC-HIGH D BLENDS

Choleric-Sanguine
This blend is more people-oriented than the other Cholerics. People with this blend are so result-oriented that they often run over others to get what they want. They easily intimidate others because of their confidence and direct method of communicating.

Choleric-Phlegmatic
This blend is more determined, unemotional and individualistic than the other Cholerics. People with this blend tend to be very cold and unresponsive to the emotional needs of others. They are very practical and "down-to-earth."

Choleric-Melancholy
This blend is more detail-oriented than the other Cholerics. People with this blend can be both cold and uncaring, or gracious and sensitive. They usually operate from a well-thought through plan. They have creative ideas and initiate change. They have command in their voice. Children are attracted to their confidence.

 ### THREE SANGUINE-HIGH I BLENDS

Sanguine-Choleric
This blend is more assertive than the other Sanguines. They are energetic, positive, and work well with and through people. They tend to be confident about their abilities and they like to lead others.

They easily and naturally influence others. They have an outgoing interest in people and have the ability to gain respect and confidence from others. People with this blend tend to assertively persuade others to their point of view.

Sanguine-Phlegmatic
This blend is more relationship-oriented than the other Sanguines. They are very approachable and place high importance on enduring relationships. They impress others with their warmth, empathy, and understanding approach. They possess a casual kind of poise in social situations. Children like them and people tend to seek them out to tell them their problems. They are well balanced and stable.

Sanguine-Melancholy
This blend is more formal than the other Sanguines. They are sensitive, emotional, and creative. They tend to be very concerned about making a favorable impression. They function best when they have a detailed plan, social contact, and time alone to think and plan. They are moody and are capable of sudden shifts in their emotions.

 ## THREE PHLEGMATIC-HIGH S BLENDS

Phlegmatic-Choleric
This blend is more industrious, determined, rigid, and unemotional than the other Phlegmatics. This persistent individual brings a deceptively intense approach to their work. Being low-key outwardly—their commitment to a task is not easily observed. People with this blend tend to be more emotionally cold and forcefully resist changing their routine.

Phlegmatic-Sanguine
This blend is more friendly than the other Phlegmatics. People with this blend tend to be too accommodating to the needs of others to the point of self-neglect. They want others to know that they have a deep desire to be of help before they can function effectively. They can be very talkative at times.

Phlegmatic-Melancholy
This blend is more consistent than the other Phlegmatics. They are routine, accommodating, and passive. Patience, control, and deliberateness characterize the usual behavior of this amiable and easy going individual.

They tend to worry and are very possessive of things, their children, and relationships. Activity tends to center around their home and family. They are very dependable and like to do one thing at a time.

 ## THREE MELANCHOLY-HIGH C BLENDS

Melancholy-Choleric

This blend is more precise and picky than the other Melancholies. Because of the secondary Choleric tendencies, they push their view as the right way. They are very attentive to detail and push to have things done correctly according to their standards. They are extremely conscientious and painstaking in work requiring accuracy and maintaining standards. They can be a perfectionist. At times they can be abrupt and abrasive.

Melancholy-Sanguine

This blend is more friendly than the other Melancholies. They have high personal ambitions. This is a well-balanced, systematic, precise thinker who tends to follow procedures in both their business and personal life. Their activity centers around their family or people with whom they are comfortable. They can be very talkative at times.

Melancholy-Phlegmatic

This blend is more conscientious and private than the other Melancholies. This quiet individual works well in a structured environment requiring attention to detail. They make decisions slowly because of collecting and analyzing information until they are sure of the right and best course of action (this is especially true when involved in a new project). They need feedback and reassurance that they have made the right decision.

INTERNAL TENSION

All temperament blend combinations experience internal tension on some level. For most of the blends, the internal tension is not a major problem. There are a few of the blends, however, who experience a more serious level of internal tension. The nature of the tension is that two temperaments representing two different and opposing forces are at work at the same time essentially pulling the person in two different directions causing tension.

THE CHOLERIC-HIGH D BLENDS

A combination of Choleric and Sanguine or Choleric and Phlegmatic tendencies do not produce significant internal conflict. The Choleric and Sanguine tendencies are both extroverted and active. There is also not much conflict when the Choleric combines with the Phlegmatic temperament because the Phlegmatic is passive and offers no resistance to the Choleric tendencies (other than slowing him/her down a little).

Internal conflict is observed when the Choleric and Melancholy are blended together. The Choleric wants to act first and the Melancholy wants to plan first. Both tendencies are focused on accomplishing the task. The Choleric side, however, wants the results quickly, and the Melancholy portion wants the right results.

If the individual learns to control both so that they plan first and then act, the internal conflict is greatly reduced and this person will become extremely focused and productive. When this is not managed well, there is instability and frequent outbursts of anger.

THE SANGUINE-HIGH I BLENDS

As with the Choleric blends, the same approach applies to the Sanguines. Not much conflict is observed when the Sanguine and Choleric are blended because both are extroverted and active. The Sanguine and Phlegmatic in combination produces very little conflict. However, great internal conflict always occurs when the Sanguine and Melancholy are in combination.

THE PHLEGMATIC-HIGH S BLENDS

When the Phlegmatic is first in combination with the other three there is generally not much internal conflict. The Phlegmatic tendency has a calming effect on the other temperaments. There is much more internal conflict, however, when the Phlegmatic is in combination with the Choleric because the Phlegmatic part will resist the push of the Choleric tendencies. The Phlegmatic and Sanguine temperaments tend to work well together although there is some conflict produced by the push of the Sanguine part on the tendency of the Phlegmatic to move slowly.

THE MELANCHOLY-HIGH C BLENDS

The greatest internal conflict for the Melancholy blends comes from the Melancholy-

Choleric combination. The primary temperament Melancholy wants to think in great detail while the Choleric part just wants results now; these two annoy each other and tend to have a war going on all the time. The other two, Melancholy-Sanguine and the Melancholy-Phlegmatic tend to work very well together with little internal conflict.

THE GREATEST INTERNAL CONFLICT

The greatest internal conflict occurs when the Sanguine is primary and the Melancholy is secondary. These two are in opposition to each other in almost every way. The Sanguine part wants to be with people and the Melancholy part wants to be alone. The Sanguine side is spontaneous and the Melancholy portion wants to plan. The Sanguine part wants to have fun and the Melancholy part wants to do something serious. The Sanguine part is disorganized and the Melancholy part is organized. The Sanguine part talks all the time and the Melancholy part speaks when it has something to say.

As you can easily see, these opposites stay at war with each other and often cause great difficulty for people hosting this blend. They are pulled in both, even opposite directions, most of the time. They often tell me they stay confused because they don't know if they should go do something with someone or think first and then make a plan!

NOTE: Those who are familiar with the DISC model will recognize that the letters I-C represent Influence (I) and Compliance (C). The I-C is the Sanguine-Melancholy. I will mostly refer to the Sanguine-Melancholy throughout this book without the accompanying letters I-C. The Letters I-C were coined from John Geier's work in the early 1970's. The terms Choleric, Sanguine, Phlegmatic, and Melancholy were coined by Galen sometime around 200 A.D.

It is important to know that the terms Sanguine and Melancholy are deeply rooted in history and not a recent concept.

02

TWELVE EARLY SIGNS

Every human has free will. Yes even your child. So each person must choose for themselves what kind of person they want to be.

TWELVE EARLY SIGNS

B efore we look at twelve signs that your child may be a Sanguine-Melancholy, here are some prenatal observations that can help identify your child's temperament even before they are born:

- The Choleric (D) baby will kick hard and abruptly
- The Sanguine (I) baby will be active and restless
- The Phlegmatic (S) baby will not be very active
- The Melancholy (C) baby will kick abruptly and be somewhat active

To illustrate, my daughter Kathy has twins, Danielle and Meagan, and before they were born, Kathy told me that one had gentle movements while the other one moved all the time and was very restless. The active one was moving and kicking almost all the time even when Kathy was trying to sleep. The gentle mover turned out to be a Melancholy (Danielle) and the active mover turned out to be a Sanguine (Meagan). The temperament of a child can be observed by how active or inactive they are while still in the womb.

The early signs of a child being a Sanguine-Melancholy are a little different from other children. Some of the following signs can be seen in some children, but if you are observing most of what follows, then the chances increase that your child has the Sanguine-Melancholy temperament.

TWELVE EARLY SIGNS

1. LACK OF SLEEP IN INFANTS

The Sanguine-Melancholy infant tends to sleep little and take short naps. They will likely be restless and not sleep through the night. When they awake they will cry loudly, usually demanding to be fed. Their restlessness will likely be noticed even in the womb. They will make their presence known with lots of movement and kicking (sometimes it will be abrupt)!

2. EARLY DEVELOPMENT

The Sanguine-Melancholy will most likely walk and talk earlier than other children. They are able to communicate at an early age to the astonishment of their parents and other adults. It's the young Sanguine-Melancholy child that performs on TV and in movies; examples are Shirley-Temple Black and Drew Barrymore. There are countless other children like these that astound us with their abilities at a very young age.

3. EMOTIONAL REACTION TO "NO"

One of the earliest revealing signs is a strong emotional reaction to being told "no." Most children do not like to hear that word but the young Sanguine-Melancholy will likely have a very strong emotional reaction when told they cannot do something. More importantly, this is also an early sign that the child is rebelling against your authority. Hearing the word "no" is usually taken personally and they feel rejected. This is a core issue and it is imperative that you delay gratification so that your child learns to respect your authority.

4. ORGANIZED

Those children who have Melancholy in their temperament, either first or second, will show early signs of being organized. It may show up in the way they line up their toys, eat their food, or dress.

When they are old enough to play with other children, they may react when another child moves a toy without their permission. After playing they may have a logical way to put away their toys and will resist another suggestion. They may even have a particular way of putting their clothes in their drawer. They may not be neat in their organization, but if they know where things are then they are organized. A two year old girl was observed lining up her shoes on the bed being very careful to put the heels to the back and the toes to the front. She also made sure the shoes were in a straight line.

5. SLOW TO WARM UP

The young Sanguine-Melancholy child is slow to warm up to new people. Children with other temperament blends are also slow to warm up to new people so this sign alone is not significant. This is revealing if the child has a high degree of the other signs. Sanguine-Melancholy children are reluctant to open up around new people until they are sure they will be accepted.

I was invited to lunch with a young couple that had a four year old Sanguine-Melancholy daughter. She was as cute as any I've seen! She was initially very shy and would look at me with a quick glance and then look away. I looked and smiled at her from across the table for about twenty minutes while I carried on a conversation with her parents. Finally she began to open up and after about thirty minutes she was making her presence known by smiling, laughing, and making a game out of eating her food. Her bright smile lit up the room and once she started talking she did not stop.

6. ANGRY OUTBURSTS

Angry outbursts over little things is another sign. The young Sanguine-Melancholy will often get angry when playing with other children and will throw toys at them or hit them or say hurtful things. This occurs after they are embarrassed, can't get their way, they feel rejected or disrespected.

I observed one young Sanguine-Melancholy before age three purposely standing on the hands of her younger cousins trying to hurt them because they were getting more attention than she was. That was one of many destructive things that child did.

A mother of a seven year old video recorded her daughter's temper-tantrum. Her daughter loudly protested screaming, "Why do you have the video camera on me?" "Crying she said, "Don't show this to anybody!" Her mother calmly said, "I'm going to show this to you later so you can see what you are doing!" The daughter quickly calmed down.

7. SENSITIVE: FEELINGS ARE EASILY HURT

Young Sanguine-Melancholies will easily get their feelings hurt over the slightest thing. Watch this happen when you take something away or do not respond quickly to what they ask for. It may also happen when you give them a firm look, ignore them, or do not say something nice about what they have done. The point is that when something happens that the young Sanguine-Melancholy takes personally it will cause him/her to react emotionally with sadness, anger, crying, or with a temper-tantrum.

8. A NEED TO BE THE CENTER OF ATTENTION

Wanting to be the center of attention is a revealing sign. If you notice your child speaking up, speaking louder, or interrupting others' conversation, it's an early sign.

The young Sanguine-Melancholy will find a way to get attention, even as an infant. They will cry until they are held and cuddled. When older, they get attention by dressing up to entertain, sing, dance, or tell a story. When the child does not get attention they may have a strong emotional reaction; they may cry, pout, or run out of the room screaming.

I was visiting a home where there were several small children present. The young boy (age 3) was making a lot of noise while playing with his toy truck. His older sister was sitting quietly at the table drawing. She was getting the attention because of her art work and her younger brother was not pleased. He began making more noise and tried to draw the attention away from his sister. His mother asked her son to stop and when he did not comply, she took his toy truck away from him. He pitched a fit! Embarrassed, he ran to the couch and buried his head under a pillow and started screaming, kicking his feet, and crying. His mother commented, "He cannot stand it if he is not the center of attention!"

9. CREATIVE EXPRESSION

A creative expression is an important sign. A young Sanguine-Melancholy may show early signs of creativity like drawing, dancing, singing, pretending to play an instrument, acting, etc. They have a very active imagination so their creativity will show up in a variety of ways. It is not unusual for them to have an imaginary friend with whom to talk and play.

Many with the Sanguine-Melancholy temperament have an exceptional talent to write at an early age. As soon as they learn to write I've known them to take a scrap of paper to their parents with a few words on it explaining that it is a story.

I was shown a letter by Bridget, a 16 year old Sanguine-Melancholy, that she had written to her father expressing her concerns and feelings about his behavior toward her that she believed was unacceptable. It was a masterful piece of work and she articulated her position clearly. It was handwritten with no corrections made! After I read the letter I remarked that this is college level writing. She later told me that her teachers often tell her about her writing ability, which she had demonstrated from an early age.

10. BRIGHT AND BORED

The Sanguine-Melancholy usually has above average intelligence. They absorb and process information very quickly. Most, but not all, that have an exceptionally high IQ are Sanguine-Melancholy. However, as they progress through the early educational years they may show signs of not being interested in learning. This may be an indication that they are bored with what is being taught or they are not being challenged by the subject matter or teacher. When they are motivated to learn, they easily outperform their peers. They are not only capable of learning quickly they are also often interested in a wide variety of subjects.

11. RADICAL BEHAVIOR AT PUBERTY

Radical behavior often occurs when a child reaches the puberty stage of life. This is true for almost everyone but when it comes to the Sanguine-Melancholy it is often more extreme. When the hormones begin to flow it can change a fairly docile child into someone that you do not recognize. Because of puberty, the intensity of feelings and desires become incredibly overwhelming for the Sanguine-Melancholy adolescent to understand or control. The first few months after the beginning of puberty can be very stormy.

12. EARLY INTEREST IN SEX

Numerous times I have dealt with young girls around age sixteen that were already sexually active. It usually starts around age fourteen with accessible boys at school or from their neighborhood. They are clever to hide their encounters and it may continue for some time before it is discovered. Once started it is very difficult to stop them from looking for an opportunity. They lie about where they are and who they are with just so they can have an encounter. Along with this activity is often experimenting with cigarettes, marijuana, and alcohol.

SEVEN THINGS TO TEACH YOUR CHILD

It is imperative that all young children are taught the following but especially the young Sanguine-Melancholy. Volumes have been written on these subjects so do some research to obtain a greater depth of understanding.

Teaching your child is only half of the formula--that is *your* responsibility. The other half is the child has to be willing to learn what is being taught--that is *their* responsibility.

Every human has free will, yes even your child. So each person must choose for themselves what kind of person they want to be. It starts early, but remember your child may or may not be willing to adhere to what you are teaching. Do your part and do it in love. Take the time to teach your child. Do not get frustrated, yell, scream, belittle or embarrass them, especially in front of others. Teach them the following in love:

1. RESPECT FOR AUTHORITY

Teach your child to do what you ask of them the first time and to do it with a good attitude. Explain the reason for your request. It's appropriate to say, "Because I ask you to." Ask only once and then address the issue if your child does not respond. Do not yell or embarrass them especially when in public. Teach them to respect your authority by saying, "Yes sir" and "Yes ma'am."

Remember that communication is not what you say, it's what the other person hears. After explaining the behavior you expect from your child say, "Tell me what you just heard me say." Have your child repeat what you said so that you are sure they understood. If they cannot give it back to you, keep explaining it until they are able to clearly state to you what you've said. Also, explain to your child the consequences to disobedience before discipline is administered. Be consistent and be sure you and your mate treat the child the same. Avoid a double standard where you say one thing and your mate says another.

Understand that without proper training at a young age, a child's lack of respect for authority will also transfer to their teachers, officers, employers or their mate.

2. YOUR EXPECTATIONS

Clearly and specifically explain what you expect from your child. Do not think that they will figure out what you want on their own. Explain to the child what is responsible, appropriate, and acceptable behavior. Explain to the child what is not responsible, appropriate, and acceptable behavior. Keep it simple, be specific, and be clear.

Without clear and specific rules to follow, the child will not know what is acceptable behavior. This causes uncertainty and confusion in the child because you will correct the child for something they did not know was unacceptable. The child will likely get angry which will bring on more correction from you and more confusion within the child. Children want to please their parents so clearly explain your expectations.

3. SELF-CONTROL

The young Sanguine-Melancholy will often demand that their needs be met immediately. They want instant gratification for all their desires and if they are not immediately satisfied, an emotional outburst usually follows. This is their attempt to manipulate you to immediately conform to their demands.

Teach your child that all gratification is not instant by waiting before fulfilling their requests. They must learn that they cannot have what they want at the moment of their request. This will help the child to develop self-control.

If an emotional outburst occurs, tell the child that when they calm down you will discuss it with them but not until. This will also teach them to delay gratification. The young Sanguine-Melancholy may say hurtful things when they cannot get what they want. This is not appropriate or acceptable behavior and if this does occur, it must be addressed immediately. Without a child learning self-control early in life means they are less likely to channel their natural abilities into a productive life as an adult.

4. NOT TO TAKE THINGS PERSONALLY

When denied something or spoken to directly or corrected, the Sanguine-Melancholy will often respond with an emotional reaction. Calmly teach the child that they have taken it personally and their response is unacceptable.

If a child is allowed to take things personally without correction, they will learn to expect everything to always go their way. This produces a selfish, self-centered adult who will have difficulties in relationships.

5. COPING SKILLS TO DEAL WITH THE FEAR OF REJECTION

The fear of rejection shows up in every aspect of the Sanguine-Melancholies' life. Their emotional outbursts and withdrawal happens when this fear is either realized or they think it may be realized. They need to be told repeatedly, in love, that what just happened is not rejection. Help them to look at it (whatever just happened) differently in a more emotionally healthy manner. See Chapter 8 for more details on how to deal with rejection.

6. TO MAKE GOOD CHOICES

My wife and I were shopping in Costco recently when a young lady passed us pushing her cart with a small child walking by her side. Suddenly an older child rushed up to her mother appearing upset and said, "Why did you leave me?" The mother calmly said to her young daughter, "Sue, I told you we were going to another part of the store. If you had made a better choice you would have stopped what you were doing and followed us." The little girl (around ten years of age) said, "You're right mom, I'm sorry."

I could not let this moment pass without a comment to the young mother. I walked up to her and said, "Excuse me, I'm a therapist and I heard what you just said to your daughter." She looked a little puzzled so I pointed out to her that she had made it clear to her daughter that she could have made a better choice. I said if all parents did that our world would be a better place. She smiled and said she appreciated my comment.

Teaching how to make good choices is paramount in helping your child develop into a mature adult. A parent of a four year old Sanguine-Melancholy told me the following story that illustrates how to teach your child about choices. She took her son to the swimming pool only to find that it was closed for the day. Her son immediately got upset and started crying. His mother told him that he had two choices: one, he could continue crying and she would take him home or two, he could stop crying and they could try to find a pool that was open. She asked him to make a choice. He decided to stop crying so they could look for a pool that was open.

When your young Sanguine-Melancholy demonstrates inappropriate behavior or gets emotional, give them options from which to choose. Simply say in love that you have two choices; you can continue what you are doing or you can stop ... and do this... What choice will you make? Sometimes you might offer more than one option from which to choose. This approach will help your child learn how to solve problems by listing options and making a choice. Without learning to make healthy choices early in life, leads one to blame their failures on other people as an adult.

7. WORK-ETHIC

The value of teaching a work-ethic to your child early in their life cannot be overstated. Proverbs 20:4, written 3,000 years ago, records the dangers of not working, "Sluggards do not plow in season; so at harvest time they look but find nothing." I've interviewed hundreds of successful people over the years and found that they all had a strong work-ethic that began between the ages of seven and twelve. Closer to age seven the stronger. They all had responsibilities around their home without being paid. They all had to clean their room, take out the trash, put the dirty dishes in the dishwasher, cut the grass, etc.

People with a work-ethic earned money in a variety of ways from having a paper-route, shoveling snow, baby-sitting, etc. One father took his five-year-old son to a creek by a golf course and together they picked up wayward golf balls from the shallow water. They would clean them and sell them to the golf course club house. One lady told me she started at age five helping her mother sell vegetables from their garden at a road-side stand in front of their home.

The money they earned was used to buy their own clothes or toys. The parents could afford to do this for their children but they wanted to teach the value of hard work and how to use and save money.

I worked at a small grocery store as a young boy and saved all the money I made to buy toys. I kept the money in a small box in my dresser drawer until I had enough for a particular toy.

I learned from my own experience and from that of others that the principle is to teach your child early to apply themselves. The core of a work-ethic is the application of one's effort to accomplish something. If a child develops a work-ethic early in life, they will carry it into their adult life and the possibility of them achieving success is greatly increased. Without a work-ethic, the chance of failure in life also greatly increases.

I also found that people who develop a work-ethic early in life became problem-solvers. Since they know how to apply themselves to work, they are more likely to apply themselves to solving life's problems.

SUMMARY

There are twelve early signs that reveal if your son or daughter may have the Sanguine-Melancholy temperament blend. Remember, the more of the twelve signs you observe in your child, the more likely your child has this blend.

The more you understand the needs of your Sanguine-Melancholy child the better you will be able to meet those needs daily. Meeting their temperament needs will reduce their frustration (and yours) and enable them to explore their creativity.

03

SELF-AWARENESS

SELF-AWARENESS

Carl Jung (1875-1961) a Swiss psychiatrist said, "Your visions will become clear only when you can look into your own heart. Who looks outside, dreams; who looks inside, awakes."

How important is self-awareness? It is what awakens us to a conscious level of understanding and acceptance of what we might not have known before. At some point during your journey through life you may have said, "I did not know that about myself." This can be either a pleasant or unpleasant experience but it should always result in personal growth.

JOHARI'S WINDOW

A helpful tool that identifies our lack of self-awareness is Johari's Window. This four-paned "window" as shown in Figure 2 divides personal awareness into four different categories. The four panes are like windows representing various levels of self-awareness: the OPEN quadrant represents things that both I know about myself and you know about me; the BLIND quadrant represents things that you know about me but I am unaware of; the HIDDEN quadrant represents things I know about myself that you do not know; the UNKNOWN quadrant represents things that neither I know about myself nor you know about me.

Johari's Window teaches that there are things about ourselves that we may not be aware of called blind spots. Before anyone can gain control over the things that may be interfering with their life, they must first become aware of their behavior.

JOHARI'S WINDOW
FIGURE 2

Known to Self **OPEN** Known to Others	Unknown to Self **BLIND** Known to Others
Known to Self **HIDDEN** Unknown to Others	Unknown to Self **UNKNOWN** Unknown to others

JOHARI'S WINDOW APPLIED

Johari's window is a key concept that will guide you toward maximizing your potential. Notice the four window panes:

OPEN

The goal is to become a more congruent person. To be congruent means that what people see on the outside represents what you are on the inside. When you are open, you are perceived to be a genuine, authentic person that does not change if the circumstances are different. For example, you are the same at a social gathering as you are at home with your family.

BLIND

There are some things about yourself that you may not see. To achieve more congruence you need to increase your self-awareness by knowing your temperament strengths and weaknesses. For example, you may talk too loud around others and not be aware of what you are doing. Be open as you read about your natural tendencies in the next chapter; it may reveal some blind spots. Once understood, choose to make the necessary corrections.

HIDDEN

There may be some things that you are concealing from others which hinders you from becoming a more congruent person. For example, you may secretly want to play a musical instrument but you keep it to yourself due to a fear of what others might think. There may be a number of things you would like to try but you are afraid of failing. Be willing to investigate what you may be hiding from others out of fear.

UNKNOWN

There are things that you do not know about yourself and others do not know about you. Be open as you investigate what it means to be a Sanguine-Melancholy. You may be pleasantly surprised at what you discover about yourself.

TEMPERAMENT AND SELF-AWARENESS

Knowing and understanding your natural temperament tendencies will increase your self-awareness of why you do what you do. Once aware, you will be able to consciously and more effectively use your natural strengths and develop a plan to overcome your natural weaknesses.

Everyone has natural strengths and natural weaknesses but not everyone is fully aware of their tendencies. The following chapter identifies the natural tendencies of the Sanguine-Melancholy temperament that are demonstrated frequently and in varying degrees. Not every Sanguine-Melancholy will have all of these characteristics nor will each one possess them to the same degree. The overall description however will represent the essence of the Sanguine-Melancholy temperament blend.

For many decades now, I have observed the incredible capabilities of people with the Sanguine-Melancholy blend. They can be and often are the best at whatever they do. When the Sanguine-Melancholy has self-awareness, self-control, and is committed to something bigger than themselves, their accomplishments are simply amazing.

As a Sanguine-Melancholy, the first step to maximizing your potential is to become aware of your natural temperament tendencies.

04

THE SANGUINE-MELANCHOLY
I-C Temperament

When they focus on goals and use their natural abilities productively, there is almost nothing they cannot accomplish.

THE SANGUINE MELANCHOLY
I-C Temperament

This chapter will cover the Sanguine-Melancholy's natural temperament tendencies. Not everyone in this group will possess all of the tendencies mentioned here nor will individuals possess these tendencies to the same degree. People vary widely in the expression of this temperament blend.

EARLY DEVELOPMENT

As discussed in Chapter 2, early development is not always true but they do have a tendency to walk, talk, and learn early and quickly. At an early age many are able to carry on a conversation with adults.

EXTROVERT AND INTROVERT

The Sanguine-Melancholy has a combination of two opposite and opposing temperaments. One is outgoing and active while the other is private and reflective. Having both the extrovert and introvert traits is often confusing to them and to those around them. They are outgoing most of the time and yet they will withdraw from people to spend time alone some of the time. They can be friendly one moment, even the life-of-the-party, and the next moment suddenly withdraw to be alone. They can be very optimistic and very pessimistic. They can have positive thoughts and then negative thoughts. They can be slow to warm up when meeting a new person or overwhelm the new person with friendliness.

PEOPLE

The Sanguine-Melancholy is mostly extroverted which means their primary need is to be with people most of the time. They are people-people. They like being with, around, or standing by others most all the time. They like to talk, play, socialize, and do most anything as long as others are there. Their need to be with people can be so great that at times they may even socialize with people they do not like!

PRIVACY

The Sanguine-Melancholy is *partly* introverted which means the secondary need is to be alone *some* of the time and to do things *right*. Daily time alone is needed, away from people, noise, or stimulation of any type. This allows time to think, analyze, and process information, or just be calm and unwind. They will likely ponder what could have happened if this had happened or consider the reason this or that did not happen, etc. To satisfy both needs to be with people and to be alone some will sit by themselves at Starbucks!

PLAN

In order to function effectively, the Sanguine-Melancholy will need a daily plan in which to operate; often it is a very detailed plan. This need comes from the Melancholy part of their temperament blend which needs alone time to plan what they will be doing the next day. By having a plan, they greatly reduce the possibility of making a mistake or failing.

CREATIVE

The Sanguine-Melancholy is the most creative of all the temperament blends and it shows up in a variety of ways. With their deep emotion and vivid imagination they may design, draw, paint, write, compose songs, write poetry, sing, dance, decorate, do woodworking, photography, etc. Those who are not involved in expressing their creativity this way tell me they do creative problem solving. Their creativity may also appear in the clothing they wear. They tend to dress fashionably and can even be flamboyant. In some way they will express their creative and colorful mind.

They are at their best when they are involved in a creative project that represents their interest. When motivated they will do as good as, if not better than, anyone else in their chosen field.

EMOTIONAL

If all emotions could be measured on a scale from one to ten, the Sanguine-Melancholy would have the entire range from top to bottom. They can express the top of the emotional scale and the bottom of the scale. This natural ability is what enables them to perform as actors and actresses.

Because they have such deep emotion, it is no surprise that they usually bring intense passion to whatever they do with their life. They feel with more intensity and depth than all the other temperament blends.

This deep well of emotion within may spontaneously erupt without warning. They can usually cry easily and often over the slightest disturbance. Surprising those around them, they may also become quickly agitated and have a strong emotional reaction.

REACTIONS TO STRESS

The Sanguine-Melancholy has a variety of reactions to stress. They may withdraw to think about the situation or talk excessively about the problem. They may get verbally or physically assertive and sarcastic. Their response to a stressful situation may also result in a sudden outburst of emotion.

FEAR OF REJECTION

The Sanguine-Melancholy has several fears all of which center around the fear of being rejected. If they perceive that they have been rejected or they are about to be rejected, it may ignite a strong emotional reaction or withdrawal.

GUILT FEELINGS

The Sanguine part of this blend is emotional and the Melancholy part of this blend wants to do things right. This easily causes the Sanguine-Melancholy to feel guilty at the slightest deviation from doing something the right way, or saying something the right way. They can be too sensitive and feel guilty about most anything but they can also rationalize away the guilt feelings.

MOOD SHIFTS

As a result of having two tendencies pulling in different directions, the Sanguine-Melancholy may experience shifts in their mood. They may rapidly change from being happy to being sad or vice versa. Mood shifts may occur when they experience guilt feelings; they withdraw to sort through their feelings and thoughts.

INTELLIGENT

The Sanguine-Melancholy tends to have above average intelligence so learning is usually effortless for them when they are motivated. They may however, drop out of the school system early because they either get bored with what is being taught, they become fearful of not passing, or they have other things they want to do besides learn. Often those who do not finish their education somehow still manage to get good paying jobs, high positions, or start their own company. If they do drop out of school, many will later get their GED. Those that develop their intellectual abilities achieve higher education. Some have told me they love learning so much that they could be a lifetime professional student.

ARTICULATE

The Sanguine-Melancholy usually has such a command of language that they can be called a word-smith (one skilled in the use of words). They can use lots of words and go into great detail with captivating stories to make a simple point. Great poets are Sanguine-Melancholy who can write and deliver soul gripping poems that mesmerize the listener.

GOOD PRESENTERS

The Sanguine-Melancholy may go to extremes to prepare for a presentation to a group by giving attention to minute details. They tend to enjoy being in front of people and being the center of attention. When the Sanguine-Melancholy uses their natural abilities effectively, they will prepare what they want to say to the group well in advance. This comes from the Melancholy part of their temperament that needs a plan. The Sanguine part of their temperament then takes over and instructs and entertains the audience with their material. They persuade others with a combination of facts and passion. This process is however usually accompanied with a high degree of performance anxiety before and after they speak.

"SIR" AND "MA'AM"

This characteristic of addressing others also has to do with image. It communicates a polite, well-mannered, proper person. By doing so, they are really asking that others show them the same respect.

PRINT

They tend to print instead of writing cursive—this is more true of male Sanguine-

Melancholies. This has to do with image because it looks better to print and it makes a better impression. I have seen some print that looks like the letters were actually typed!

JOURNAL

This tends to be more of a female trait than male, although I have known of males to keep a journal. There appears to be a need to record the events of their life so they write down their thoughts and feelings about events and people. Sometimes this is expressed as poetry and some even write songs. The poetry is usually full of deep emotion revealing the depth of the pain they are feeling.

COOKING

When this is true, they will usually do it with a bit of flair, even gourmet style. Not only will the food taste great, but the plate will look so appealing and be so artistically presented that it will look too good to eat!

GUITAR

It is not unusual for them to play (or want to play) the guitar because it makes them the center of attention.

FISHING

The Sanguine-Melancholy often uses fishing to get their alone time. It gives them time away from others and their day-to-day activities allowing them time to think and feed their analytical side or to just enjoy being alone. They may also have a fishing buddy so they are not completely isolated from people.

CLOTHING

How they appear to others can be so important to them that the Sanguine-Melancholy will be picky about the way they dress. They have a tendency to dress fashionably and can be very flamboyant. Males sometimes wear pants and shirts that are starched and females like wearing high heels. They seem to favor the color black. They often prefer clothing that represents status and quality. They may overspend just to have a status symbol or the best quality.

They are apt to place so much importance on clothing that their closet may be well organized. I've been told by many Sanguine-Melancholies that they arrange their clothing according to types and color and according to what day of the week they are to be worn.

HAIR

The male Sanguine-Melancholy will often have a beard or mustache which is usually trimmed neatly. It is also not unusual to see males with longer hair. Females may go to the other extreme and shave their head to draw attention to themselves (this is usually during the younger years) or change their hair color to something unusual; as it has shock value and draws attention. Of course not all will go to these extremes but when it happens, it is almost always the Sanguine-Melancholy.

ENTREPRENEURIAL

The Sanguine-Melancholy seems to naturally have an entrepreneurial spirit that shows their creative mind and clever insight expressing new and innovative ideas. Consider Steve Jobs that gave us the iPhone and Thomas Kinkade that made a fortune off of copies of his creative paintings. They have been successful in restaurants, clothing lines, software development, video games, etc.

The Sanguine-Melancholy needs to have a well-thought through plan before launching their idea to be in the best possible position to be successful.

SLEEP

The mind of the Sanguine-Melancholy is very active and never seems to stop processing information so they have difficulty going to sleep and staying asleep. One told me that, "Thoughts are flying around in my head like the ball in a pinball machine and my mind lights up the score board with thoughts."

They are thinking about the day, planning tomorrow, pondering why this or that happened, investigating what might happen, and even trying to figure out what to do if this or that were to happen. They tend to analyze everything that happens to them or about them, then they will analyze what they have just analyzed! Sleep will be discussed more in Chapter 18.

SENSUAL

They have a vivid imagination and lots of deep emotion. Frequently the result of this combination is sensuality. They love to be touched and caressed but only on their terms.

TATTOOS

Of course not all will be attracted to having tattoos, but some will have at least a small one placed in a slightly noticeable spot. Others on the other hand, will have multiple tattoos that are quite visible.

GYM

It is not unusual for the Sanguine-Melancholy (especially males) to spend a lot of time at the gym. Many are attracted to body building and become personal trainers.

MARRIAGE

The Sanguine-Melancholy often marries a passive person. This kind of person tends to calm them down just by being in their presence. The passive person tends to tolerate their mood shifts and behavior better than a more assertive person. This type of marriage tends to last. The marriage between two Sanguine-Melancholies is almost always filled with tension, frustration, and arguments until they learn to have mutual respect for each other.

THRILL SEEKING

Since the Sanguine-Melancholy has the entire range of human emotion, it is no surprise that some seek experiences that give them an emotional thrill.

On the lighter side
The motorcycle is a favorite choice because of the freedom it gives and the stimulation of the wind blowing in their face. Some like to join bike clubs to be with those of like mind. An open air Jeep is another favorite because it allows the air to rush over their face and it looks "cool." They tend to like the thrill of speed in any kind of vehicle because of the adrenaline rush.

On the extreme side
Some seek physical, sexual, and financial risks for the thrill and the adrenaline rush. They may ignore, tolerate, or minimize the risk of harm in exchange for

the excitement of the activity. Just how much stimulation satisfies varies with the individual. If the activity produces an acceptable level of excitement the more likely the activity will be repeated to seek an even higher level of excitement.

I realize that some of this behavior is extreme and many do not go this far, but it does happen. I've had many tell me that they experimented with these kinds of activities until something dramatic happened that changed the course of their life and they stopped.

SUDDEN BLUNTNESS AND INTENSITY

The Sanguine-Melancholy can suddenly become blunt and intense. Anyone, regardless of their temperament blend, can have a sudden burst of assertiveness or aggression and be blunt. This can be caused by anger or the need to protect oneself from sudden danger. For example, everyone is armed with the fight-or-flight response potential which is a physiological reaction that occurs in response to a perceived harmful event, attack, or threat. There is, however, another possibility.

Some with the Sanguine-Melancholy blend have Choleric (D) as their third temperament while others have Phlegmatic (S) as their third. There is a difference. When the Phlegmatic is third, the person is usually more docile, less intense, and less assertive. When the Choleric is third, the person is more driven to get results and will be more direct, intense, and blunt in communication.

Drive
The Sanguine-Melancholy-Choleric (I/C/D) has a more intense drive to get results. This combination is more naturally active, assertive, and direct.

Bluntness
When the Sanguine-Melancholy temperament is followed by the Choleric (D), then a frequent display of assertiveness or bluntness is common to make a point. This not only surprises the one on the receiving end of the sudden bluntness, but also the one delivering the message.

When the Choleric temperament is third, it represents an emotional punch. Of course, I am not referring to a physical punch but a sudden blunt response of words or emotion is possible. The presence of the Choleric temperament forces what is in front of it (the Sanguine and Melancholy) to make a point and to get results. When this happens, it is almost always offensive to the one receiving the blunt message because it is sudden and it does not represent the normal demeanor of the Sanguine-Melancholy, thus the surprise by both parties. If this is your behavior frequently, then you likely have Choleric as your third temperament. Once aware, make a conscious effort to control the sudden expression of a point so that it is not offensive. Be calm and matter-of-fact.

There is a difference between an angry display and being direct and blunt. Anger is an emotion related to one's interpretation of having been offended, wronged, or denied and an attempt to retaliate. A blunt response communicates sudden directness to make a point.

SUMMARY

These are the tendencies and traits that the Sanguine Melancholy will demonstrate frequently in varying degrees. It must be pointed out again that not every Sanguine-Melancholy will have all of these characteristics nor will each one possess them to the same degree. The overall description however, represents the essence of the Sanguine-Melancholy temperament blend.

The Sanguine-Melancholy is an intelligent, gifted, creative, and multi-talented person. You are able to create innovative and pleasing things with your creative thinking. When you focus on goals and use your natural abilities productively, there is almost nothing you cannot accomplish.

HOW TO MAXIMIZE YOUR POTENTIAL

Because Your Impact Is Great

Every temperament blend has natural strengths and natural weaknesses. Success in life is directly related to how well you develop and use your natural strengths and overcome your natural weaknesses. The coming chapters will include proven tools and practices that you can apply in your every day life so that your potential as a Sanguine-Melancholy can be realized at its fullest. As one of the most capable temperament blends, the realization of your potential not only means opened possibilities for you, but also for those around you. As you go on this journey, all you are asked to do is to practice, don't worry about failure, the only way you fail is by doing nothing.

05

BE WITH PEOPLE

BE WITH PEOPLE

As a Sanguine-Melancholy, your strength is that you are mostly a "people person." To be at your best, you need to spend most of the time with people. Since you are naturally attracted to be with, by, or around others most of the time, you enjoy interacting, talking, laughing, and having fun. You like groups, parties, sporting events or anywhere others are gathered. You have a natural smile and tend to talk a lot (the subject matter of the conversation is not that important). To want to be with people socially and professionally is normal and natural and it's when you feel your best.

Your extroverted Sanguine side not only needs to be with people but it also needs to be active and doing exciting activities. Since this is your biggest need, it is easy to create opportunities for the Sanguine part to be expressed by being with people, playing, and having some fun. Enjoy the Sanguine side of your temperament.

WHAT CAN YOU DO?

BE AWARE

Be aware that you have a need to be with people socially and professionally. Your primary temperament is Sanguine which means you have a natural desire to be around others most of the time. This is a strong temperament need which is not only normal, it is compelling. You cannot deny nor neglect this need for very long without having an uneasy feeling. If denied or neglected, you may even feel a little irritated and may not feel good about yourself.

The uneasy feeling you get is to alert you of your need for people contact. It is easily satisfied when you make time with another person or simply talk to someone on the phone. Be aware that you are at your best when you are around other people relating and having fun.

TAKE CONTROL

To maximize your potential, be sure you have regular contact with others in order to meet your need to be with people.

06

SPEND TIME ALONE

It's an interesting combination: Having a great fear of being alone, and having a desperate need for solitude and the solitary experience. That's always been a tug of war for me.

-JODIE FOSTER | ACTRESS

SPEND TIME ALONE

As a Sanguine-Melancholy, you have a need to be with people most of the time. The introverted side of your temperament blend however, needs to be alone some of the time to think, create, plan, or just review the activities and events of the day. This need is so powerful that if neglected it will cause internal tension and you will feel agitated, anxious, and even angry which usually results in a noticeable shift in your mood.

It may sound strange but I have had many with this blend say to me that they felt guilty spending time alone because they thought that it was selfish. Please know that it is *not selfish*, it is in the *best interest of self* to spend time alone. So give yourself permission each day to spend as much time alone as you need.

How much alone time you need depends on what is going on in your life. Some alone time is required every day just to review what happened that day and to plan what you are going to do tomorrow. The amount of time can be anywhere from thirty minutes to an hour or more. If however there is a problem you're trying to solve or there was abnormal stress during the day, then you may need more time to process your thoughts. Even more alone time is needed when a creative moment hits and your mind is flooded with ideas and possibilities.

Alone time doesn't necessarily mean sitting in a room by yourself although many find that relaxing. Alone time can be achieved when you are exercising, riding a bike or motorcycle, hiking, swimming, fishing, cooking, taking a walk, drinking coffee at a coffee shop, etc. Some use their commute to and from work to process their thoughts.

Listening to soft music during your alone time can also help you relax as you process your thoughts. The key is to give yourself enough alone time so that you are mentally satisfied. Your mind and body will let you know when you've had enough alone time and you're ready to let the Sanguine part come out to be with people and socialize.

When discussing the need to be alone with the Sanguine-Melancholy, many will immediately agree and explain in great detail how they go about getting their private time. There are some, however, that will disagree that they ever spend time alone. When I meet resistance I usually probe their daily routine. What I find is that if they commute to work they usually do so alone and will not play the radio or a listen to a CD. They will think about the upcoming day, what they will do, what they will say, etc. Others have told me that they have trouble going to sleep and staying asleep because they are thinking about something. Others will stay up late at night just to surf the TV channels or the Internet. One Sanguine-Melancholy told me that when he is at work he takes his lunch break in his car each day in order to be alone. The point is that people with this temperament blend need to be alone to process their thoughts or just be away from people. As a Sanguine-Melancholy, if you do not get regular time alone, you will not feel good about yourself or function at a high level.

A young married man did not get daily alone time on a regular basis so he would reach a point when he could not take it any longer and he would disappear for a week at a time. No one knew where he was staying not even his wife. Turns out he would rent a motel room to simply sit, think, and enjoy being by himself. After he got caught up on his need for private time he would go back to his wife and children. Of course this was an inappropriate way to meet his need to be alone but this had been his pattern for fifteen years.

An older gentleman told me that he was not feeling very well and that he had lost his motivation. This was critical because he was in a very demanding sales job and he would not be able to pay his bills without selling. He was confused, tired, and overwhelmed, and he was not selling. I had only one question for this Sanguine-Melancholy salesman. I asked him when was the last time he had spent time alone "doing his thing." His response was, "I can't remember the last time I did anything for myself." I asked him what was his most enjoyable activity and he said that he really enjoyed working in his garden. I suggested that he do that as much as he could over the coming weekend. On Monday morning he called to say he felt like a new person. The problem was that he had neglected his "alone time" and his body and mind would not give him peace. As soon as he met his basic temperament need to be alone he relaxed and life was good again. Over the next few weeks his sales went up dramatically.

WHAT CAN YOU DO?

BE AWARE

Be aware that you have a need for alone time. Your secondary temperament is Melancholy which means you have a natural desire to have some alone time every day. This is a strong temperament need and it is not only normal but it is also very compelling.

You cannot deny nor neglect your need to be with people nor can you deny or neglect your need to be alone without having an uneasy feeling. If you do not have alone time every day you will not feel well. The uneasy feeling you get is to alert you that your need to be with people has been satisfied for now and you need some alone time. This need will be satisfied when you remove yourself from other people to be alone to think, plan, review, and to be creative. This need is so powerful that it is not possible for you to function effectively without sufficient alone time.

TAKE CONTROL

To maximize your potential, take control of this important need and be sure you have regular alone time every day. Consciously be in control to obtain balance between being with people and being alone. Pay attention to what your mind and body are telling you. Both will let you know when it's time to be with people and when it's time to be alone.

GIVE YOURSELF PERMISSION TO BE ALONE

Your temperament blend is designed to spend time away from people just to be alone so you can reflect. Remember that this is not selfish. It is in your best interest to spend time alone. Remember also that when you've had enough alone time, your mind and body will let you know that's it's time to be with people again.

CAUTION

Since your biggest need is to be with people, you may spend too much time being with others to the neglect of your need to be alone. It's like when you are enjoying a good meal and you find it hard to stop eating. You know you should but it's so tasty that you just keep on eating and eating! Later you admit that you should have stopped when you first felt full. Being with people can be so enjoyable that it is difficult to walk away from having a fun time.

Remember when you need to be alone you will begin to feel uneasy and uncomfortable around others. This is the signal that your need to be alone has been activated. Find some alone time as soon as it is reasonable to do so.

SEEK BALANCE

The need for balance in this area is critical. I cannot stress enough the importance that you regulate your time with people and being alone. Neither one can be denied or neglected without the internal consequences of stress, tension, and irritability. When both of these needs are met on a consistent basis you will feel less stress and more peaceful. Remember, the need to be with people and to be alone is natural, normal, and necessary.

07

OPERATE FROM A PLAN

OPERATE FROM A PLAN

A s previously discussed, you must have alone time every day. It's during that time that you carefully consider and plan what you are going to do the next day.

As a Sanguine-Melancholy you cannot operate effectively without a detailed plan for each day. To try to operate without a plan is like driving a car with an engine malfunction that causes the engine to "sputter." Today's cars are equipped with a warning light that alerts us that there is a problem with the engine. You do not ignore that warning light because the engine is no longer running smoothly so you take action to get it fixed. Without a well thought through plan you will "sputter" throughout the day. When you recognize that you are "sputtering" (an uneasy feeling) that is your warning light that you are trying to operate without a plan for the day. Give attention to the warning light (the uneasy feeling) and stop what you are doing and think through the rest of the day. You cannot neglect the need for a plan without consequences. Plan ahead every day what you are going to do, when you are going to do it, how you are going to do it, etc.

This is one of the most common areas of neglect that I address when working with the Sanguine-Melancholy. Many tell me that they are so busy that they do not have time for themselves. If you are saying that, then you are too busy. You must take time out each day to be alone and plan.

WHAT CAN YOU DO?

BE AWARE

You need to have a plan on which to operate every day. The better the plan the better you will feel about yourself and the less anxiety (sputtering) you will experience.

Be aware that the Sanguine part of your temperament needs spontaneity which conflicts with the need to have a plan. One Sanguine-Melancholy told me that his plan was to not have a plan for the weekends so he could be spontaneous! His plan was to not have a plan. He was self-aware and took steps to meet both of his needs to have a plan and to be spontaneous.

There will be times when you may not need a plan due to a day off from work or being on vacation, etc. In these cases, you can plan to not have a plan and that becomes your plan! This is a necessary mental exercise because the Melancholy part of your temperament blend will always be pulling on you to have a plan. Be good to yourself and set time aside every day to plan what you are going to do the next day even if you are not going to do anything.

TAKE CONTROL

To maximize your potential, take control of this important need and be sure you take the time each day to formulate a plan for the next day. The key for the Sanguine-Melancholy is to *always* do this. Once you are familiar and comfortable with your daily activities, then having a detailed plan is not as vital.

The *most* important time to have a detailed plan and time alone is when you are going to do something you have not experienced before--such as a job interview, starting a new project, or making a presentation. You will need to spend more alone time to think through and plan what you are about to experience. Let the important people in your life know that you will be spending more time alone to prepare for the upcoming event so they will understand.

As a Sanguine-Melancholy, when you do not consistently take the time to develop a daily plan, you are likely to become confused, anxious, and irritable. Some seek outside help and medication because they do not understand why they feel so nervous and agitated. It's a plan that is needed not medication. Have a plan each day on which to operate and you will not feel confused and anxious. There is a direct correlation between having a plan and having internal peace.

08

DEVELOP COPING SKILLS

People are disturbed, not by things or events but by the views (perceptions) which they take of them.

-EPICTETUS | STOIC PHILOSOPHER

DEVELOP COPING SKILLS

The Sanguine-Melancholy has enormous potential and is a creative genius in whatever field they choose. What prevents you from achieving your potential is you do not conquer your fears and you may often experience depression. I have worked with Sanguine-Melancholies since the 1970's and these are two major areas that most every one struggles to deal with effectively. Unless these two areas are conquered with coping skills, your great ability and potential will not be realized.

EIGHT FEARS THAT WILL PREVENT YOU FROM MAXIMIZING YOUR POTENTIAL

The Sanguine-Melancholy possesses the entire range of human emotion from top to bottom. It is out of their deep well of emotion that comes the passion that feeds their creativity. I heard a fourteen year old girl sing a very passionate song that she had written. Those judging the audition were amazed at the insight and passion she had at such a young age; she could not have possibly had the experience she sang about at her age. When asked how she did that, she responded that she watched a lot of movies! Because of her emotional depth, she was able to identify with the pain she saw in the movies.

Because of your emotional and sensitive nature, you may struggle with fears that may prevent you from maximizing your potential. Let's take a closer look at some of the most common fears.

BEING REJECTED

The fear of rejection is such a powerful issue that I find that most everything that is going on in the life of a Sanguine-Melancholy is almost always related to it in some way. They may cling to others to avoid even the slightest possibility of rejection. It may also be difficult to let go of a bad relationship just to avoid the feeling of rejection. Some build a wall around them that prevents anyone from getting too close.

Many have said to me that they are people pleasers explaining that it is hard to say no to a request from someone. This usually means they are trying to avoid looking unfavorably to others so they say yes to almost anything. This never works because the individual will become frustrated with themselves because they will do things they really do not want to do.

The fear of rejection may so grip the Sanguine-Melancholy that it prevents intimacy with their partner or getting too close to another person. If they do, they fear that the other person may reject them for some reason (like finding out what they are really like) and that pain would be too difficult to accept. The old saying that it is better to have loved and lost than to not have loved at all is not accepted.

NOT BEING RESPECTED

The Sanguine-Melancholy wants to be respected. A very sensitive Sanguine-Melancholy will easily take things personally and may react with strong negative emotion.

BEING EMBARRASSED

The Sanguine-Melancholy can be so self-conscious that they feel uneasy at the slightest indication that they have made a mistake (or may make a mistake), are the object of someone's joke, or are being upstaged. Consequently, they can be easily embarrassed--feeling the pain deeply.

A rookie salesperson told me about being on a sales call with his manager. The idea was for the manager to make the presentation and the rookie was to only observe. During the presentation the rookie became eager to participate. While the sales manager was making a point, the rookie simply added what he thought was an appropriate comment. The sales manager suddenly became embarrassed at the interruption. As soon as they left the building the sales manager turned to the rookie with a look that frightened him. With hate and rage in his eyes he said, "Don't you EVER do that to me again!"

During a family gathering at a park a teenage Sanguine-Melancholy was asked to get something that was about one hundred feet away. Lots of people were standing around talking in small groups. The young Sanguine-Melancholy was so self-conscious she said, "I am not going to walk in front of all those people because they will look at me!"

FAILING

Sometimes the fear of failing is so great that they may not even try to accomplish a task. If this fear is not dealt with, they may do extreme things to avoid the slightest possibility of failing.

In school, the Sanguine-Melancholy may not want to go back to class because of this fear—they may be afraid that the teacher will ask a question and they will not know the answer. Some never finish college for this reason. Others string out their college career for years because of this fear.

When at play, this fear often makes it difficult for the Sanguine-Melancholy to enjoy the sport of the game. A young man told me he would not play one-on-one basketball with his brother in the backyard because he was afraid he would lose the game.

NOT BEING IN CONTROL

One of the ways the Sanguine-Melancholy attempts to avoid the possibility of being rejected or looking bad to others is by being in control. They think that if they can control people and events then their risk of being rejected is greatly reduced.

NOT BEING WELL RECEIVED

They have such a deep need to make a favorable impression that they can be overly concerned about how well they are being received, how well people are responding to them, or what others are thinking about them. Thoughts like: *"Do they like me?" "How am I doing?" "Did I say the right thing?" "How does my hair look?"* rush through their mind when with people--especially someone they've just met. In an uncomfortable situation, the Sanguine-Melancholy may act more aloof and formal which is an attempt at putting a wall up to protect themselves from rejection. This fear of not being well-received causes a tendency to be nervous around people. When male Sanguine-Melancholies are overly concerned about being well received, it causes their palms to become clammy.

BEING SUCCESSFUL

As odd as this may sound, they sometimes fear success. The fear is that if they are successful then others will expect it to continue and they may not be able to perform at the same level.

NOT BEING IMPORTANT

Sometimes the Sanguine-Melancholy just wants to *be* important, they do not want to *do* something important. They may seek titles, positions, and power so they can project an air of importance. They do not want to actually earn importance; they just want to appear to be important. This is ironic because they are capable of achieving high success when they apply their natural, creative abilities.

WHAT CAN YOU DO?

As a Sanguine-Melancholy, if you identify with any of the fears mentioned then here are some things you can do to prevent these fears from interfering with your life. To gain control over your fears that may be preventing you from achieving your maximum potential consider the following:

BE AWARE

Become aware that your fears may be interfering with maximizing your potential. Realize that it is normal to be fearful because of your sensitive and emotional nature.

TAKE CONTROL

To maximize your potential, decide now to develop effective coping skills to deal with your fears. You have two choices: You can continue to give in to your fears allowing them to control you or you can develop coping skills to overcome them.

The idea in developing coping skills is to plan ahead so that you are ready when the difficult moments occur. As a boy scout, we were taught to be prepared for anything when we went for our overnight trips--for rain, for heat, for whatever may come. The more equipped you are, the better chance you'll survive and enjoy. As a Sanguine-Melancholy, you will need to equip yourself the same way!

Over the years I have seen many Sanguine-Melancholies get derailed by their fears because they never planned ahead to deal with a difficult moment. Without being prepared, most will react the same way they have in the past and get the same results. As a Sanguine-Melancholy, if you want different results than what you have been getting, try something different. Decide ahead of time what you are going to do when life slaps you in the face or throws you a curve.

In 1980 John Lennon released a song called "Beautiful Boy" with the following lyrics; "Life is what happens to you while you're busy making other plans." How profound! Life does have surprises and disappointments when you least expect it. You need to be prepared to meet them by planning ahead what you are going to do.

OVERCOME YOUR FEARS

The following outline will help you think through each issue that causes fear and anxiety. Those that are controlled by these emotions avoid facing the issue because they think the pain will be too great.

It is possible to overcome the control that a particular fear has over you and it is possible to overcome situations that produce anxiety. The idea is to plan ahead by thinking through what causes you to become fearful and anxious and decide in advance what action you are going to take.

It begins with identifying what is causing you difficulty. This may sound simple but it may actually be quite difficult. When I ask a client, "What are you afraid of?" they will most often say, "I'm not sure." I get the same answer when I ask, "What causes you to have anxiety?" You can solve a problem only after it's been identified. Follow the outline below to break the grip that fear has over you:

Step 1
Clearly identify your fear or what situation causes you to become anxious. Write out your conclusions. Keep writing until you have exhausted your thoughts and the fear or situation is clearly identified. Be very specific.

Step 2
Answer this question, "What is the worst that could happen if my fear or anxiety is realized?" Write down everything you think might happen. Be specific.

Step 3
Probe the question, "What is the probability of coping if the worst happened? Is it possible or impossible?" If you think it is impossible, explain why.

Step 4
Write down at least three ways to cope with your fear or anxiety. Get creative. What have you seen others do to cope?

Step 5
Explore this question, "Is my fear or anxiety exaggerated?" Yes or no?

Step 6
Think about this question, "Have I underestimated my ability to cope with this fear or anxiety?" Yes or no?

Step 7
Answer this question, "Which of the following is the most effective way to deal with my fear or anxiety:"

     ☐ Do nothing different
     ☐ Face my fear or anxiety until it is conquered

Fill in the outline for each fear or situation you identify. Face your fears by deciding to put into practice what you have written. If you practice this, you will discover that fear no longer has power over your emotions. If you practice it long enough you will no longer experience anxiety.

OVERCOME YOUR FEAR OF REJECTION

The fear of rejection is such a core issue that it requires special attention. It is this fear that has the greatest hold on you and causes you the greatest difficulty. Work through the following outline to overcome your fear of being rejected or if you have been rejected:

Step 1:   *What is my fear?*
               Answer: _____ may reject me.

Step 2:   *What is the worst that could happen if my fear is realized?*
               Answer: _____ would no longer want to be associated with me.

Step 3:   *What is the probability of coping if the worst were to happen?*
               Answer: It is possible to cope.

Step 4:   *Here are three ways to cope with my fear:*

I WILL NOT TAKE IT PERSONALLY
Relationships fail for any number of reasons. Sometimes a relationship just does not work and I do not have to know why. It doesn't mean that I'm a bad person or that I have to make the other person pay for the choice they made.

I WILL LEARN FROM THIS EXPERIENCE
I will write down what I have gained and what I have learned from the relationship. People enter our lives for a reason, season, or a lifetime. See the poem at the end of this chapter.

I WILL MOVE ON WITH MY LIFE
When failures happen, and they happen to everyone, I will not linger long before I move on with my life. I will not look back.

Step 5:   *Is my fear or anxiety exaggerated?"*
Answer: <u>Yes.</u>

Step 6:   *Have I underestimated my ability to cope with this fear?*
Answer: <u>Yes.</u>

Step 7:   *I have conquered my fear of being rejected by facing it and deciding to let it go and move on with my life.*

DEPRESSION

What is depression? Depression is a feeling of sadness and dejection that alters a person's emotional and mental state and interferes with their daily life functions in varying degrees. Symptoms range from mild to severe and can be short term or last for an extended period of time.

WHAT ARE THE SYMPTOMS OF DEPRESSION?

According to the National Institute of Mental Health, the following are the symptoms of depression ("Signs & Symptoms," n.d.):

- Persistent sad, anxious, or "empty" feelings
- Feelings of hopelessness or pessimism
- Feelings of guilt, worthlessness, or helplessness
- Irritability, restlessness
- Loss of interest in activities or hobbies once pleasurable, including sex
- Fatigue and decreased energy
- Difficulty concentrating, remembering details, and making decisions
- Insomnia, early-morning wakefulness, or excessive sleeping
- Overeating, or appetite loss
- Thoughts of suicide, suicide attempts
- Aches or pains, headaches, cramps, or digestive problems that do not ease even with treatment.

WHAT CAUSES DEPRESSION?

According to the National Institute of Mental Health, the medical explanation for the cause of depression is as follows ("Causes," n.d.):

Most likely, depression is caused by a combination of genetic, biological, environmental, and psychological factors.

Depressive illnesses are disorders of the brain. Brain-imaging technologies, such as magnetic resonance imaging (MRI), have shown that the brains of people who have depression look different than those of people without depression. The parts of the brain involved in mood, thinking, sleep, appetite, and behavior appear different. **But these images do not reveal why the depression has occurred. They also cannot be used to diagnose depression.**

Some types of depression tend to run in families. However, depression can occur in people without family histories of depression too. Scientists are studying certain genes that may make some people more prone to depression. Some genetics research indicates that risk for depression results from the influence of several genes acting together with environmental or other factors. In addition, trauma, loss of a loved one, a difficult relationship, or any stressful situation may trigger a depressive episode. Other depressive episodes may occur with or without an obvious trigger.

According to the excerpt above (emphasis, mine), the medical community is still not clear as to what is truly the cause of depression. They hypothesize that it is somewhere between nature and nurture.

STANDARD MEDICAL TREATMENT FOR DEPRESSION

The medical profession uses medication to treat depression. According to Medical News Today, "the aim of an antidepressant is to stabilize and normalize the neurotransmitters in our brain (naturally occurring brain chemicals), such as serotonin, dopamine, and neonepherin. According to various studies, these neurotransmitters play a vital role in regulating mood. We know they regulate mood but we are not exactly sure how they do it" (Nordqvist, n.d.).

ANOTHER VIEW OF DEPRESSION

Everyone will experience disappointing events during their life that will challenge their mental and emotional state of equilibrium. It is human to feel sadness and remorse when such events occur. There is a normal period of adjustment that it takes to regain our usual mental and emotional sense of well-being. Not everyone that experiences depression will ask for medication to relieve their symptoms. The fields of medicine and psychology hold that the underlying cause of depression is a chemical imbalance in the brain. Let's consider another way of looking at the cause and cure of depression.

Epictetus (AD 55–135), a stoic philosopher said, **"People are disturbed, not by things or events but by the views (perceptions) which they take of them."** It is my view that this is the best explanation of what we are calling depression that I have seen. Simply put, people disturb themselves.

In all my years as a therapist I have never seen a happy depressed person! People that come to me with the symptoms of depression are dealing with a disappointing life event. I have never dealt with anyone that reported symptoms of depression who was unable to identify an event that was causing their emotional pain. When I point out that they are thinking too much about the wrong thing everyone immediately agrees.

The issue is not something that their brain is doing to them because of the lack of brain chemistry balance, it is because they are disturbing themselves by negative thinking. People get stuck and they do not have an effective coping skill to get beyond the disturbing event that has occurred.

When there is a catastrophic life changing event there will be great sadness and deep feelings of loss. This is a normal human experience. People who have healthy coping skills recover from a disappointing life event in a reasonable amount of time without the use of medication. Those with healthy coping skills tend to be problem solvers who look for ways to overcome obstacles in order to move on with their life. People that battle depression are frequently not good at solving problems

WHAT CAN YOU DO?

As a Sanguine-Melancholy, if you struggle with depression on occasion, here are some things you can do:

BE AWARE

Be aware that when you are feeling sad or dejected *that you are thinking too much about the wrong thing.* You are not trying to solve the problem, rather you are stuck looking at the problem and not on the solution to the problem.

TAKE CONTROL

To maximize your potential, decide to take control of the way you are thinking that leads you to get depressed. You have two choices: You can continue to give into your negative thoughts allowing them to control you or you can decide to look at the situation differently.

DEAL WITH THE CAUSE OF DEPRESSION

According to Epictetus, what disturbs people is not what happens but what they think about what happens to them. It's not the event; it's what the individual thinks about the event--people disturb themselves by the way they view (or perceive) people and events. Based on the statement that Epictetus made, use the ABC approach shown below to live more effectively and above the circumstances of life by choosing to change your perception so that you are not disturbed.

The ABC's of life

A - "Men are disturbed not by things or events but by the views
      (perceptions) which they take of them"
B - Since it is my view (perception) that causes me to be disturbed...
C - What should my view (perception) be so that I am not disturbed.

Let's apply this concept to the content of this book. Here's how it works: as a Sanguine-Melancholy, you may think it is bad to be rejected, embarrassed, fail, lose, not be important, not be well received, be put down, look badly in the eyes of others, and to not be respected. You think these things are bad and therefore have a negative reaction when any of these occur. You either get angry or anxious, lose control of your emotions, or get depressed.

It's critical to understand that it is not the event that is disturbing you, it's what you think about the event that is causing you to be disturbed. If you were to apply this outline, you would eventually gain complete control over anything that disturbs you.

Consider changing what you think from "being rejected is a bad thing" to "being rejected is a common experience in life and I can learn something from the experience." If you changed your thinking to "this relationship was not meant to be" then you will not feel that being rejected is a bad thing and that it only happens to you. Rejection happens to everyone.

Consciously and willfully think about what is disturbing you. Write it down. Consciously and willfully think about another way of looking at what is disturbing you. If you were to change your view (perception) of the person or the event, you would not be disturbed nor would you need medication to calm you down. **Medication will do for you what you will not do for yourself.**

Ask this question, *"How can I look at this so it's not a problem?"* Now consider as many options as you can think of to solve the problem that you are facing. The solutions must be moral and ethical. After you have written down the possible solutions to the problem, take some time and carefully consider each possibility. Now choose the one solution that will most effectively solve the problem. The more you use this process, the less attention you will be giving to the disappointing event.

Sometimes people take an inordinate amount of time to adjust to a disturbing event. Again, there is a normal adjustment time necessary to regain our usual emotional state when a disappointing event occurs. Work at it until you reduce your reaction time to the point that you do not react but rather you respond immediately with a healthy choice.

A REASON. A SEASON. A LIFETIME
(Author Unknown)

People always come into your life for a reason, a season, or a lifetime.
When you figure out which it is, you know exactly what to do.
When someone is in your life for a REASON,
It is usually to meet a need you have expressed
outwardly or inwardly.
They have come to assist you through a difficulty,
Or to provide you with guidance and support,
To aid you physically, emotionally, or even spiritually.
They may seem like a godsend to you, and they are.
They are there for the reason you need them to be.
Then, without any wrong doing on your part
or at an inconvenient time,
This person will say or do something
to bring the relationship to an end.
Sometimes they die. Sometimes they just walk away.
Sometimes they act up and force you to take a stand.
What we must realize is that our need has been met,
our desire fulfilled; their work is done.
The prayer you sent up has been answered
and it is now time to move on.
When people come into your life for a SEASON,
It is because your turn has come to share, grow, or learn.
They may bring you an experience of peace or make you laugh.
They may teach you something you have never done.
They usually give you an unbelievable amount of joy.
Believe it! It is real! But, only for a season.
And like Spring turns to Summer and Summer to Fall,
The season eventually ends.
LIFETIME relationships teach you lifetime lessons;
Those things you must build upon in order to have
a solid emotional foundation.
Your job is to accept the lesson, love the person anyway;
And put what you have learned to use in all other
relationships and areas in your life.
It is said that love is blind but friendship is clairvoyant.
Thank you for being part of my life,
Whether you were a reason, a season or a lifetime.

09

CONTROL YOUR THOUGHTS & EMOTIONS

CONTROL YOUR THOUGHTS & EMOTIONS

The Sanguine-Melancholy temperament is a unique blend of two opposite and opposing tendencies that combine to produce a fast thinking and emotional person. No other temperament blend is composed quite like this one.

THOUGHTS

As a result of this unique blend, the Sanguine-Melancholy can experience so many thoughts at the same time that it seems like a fireworks display on the fourth-of-July happening in their mind. Thoughts can race quickly into and out of their mind representing opposite, even opposing ideas. They can take one thought in many different directions exploring what it means, what it could mean, what it doesn't mean, why it means anything, what about this, what about that, what are the possibilities, and on and on it goes with no end in sight! Many have said they feel overwhelmed and can't seem to stop or manage the avalanche of thoughts.

EMOTIONS

It is an understatement to say that the Sanguine-Melancholy can be emotional. Remember this blend possesses the entire range of human emotion from top to bottom. So they are capable of feeling intense emotion about what happens in their life. No other temperament blend has the amount and intensity of emotion as does this one which is why they can laugh, get angry, or cry easily and often. It is because of this that they can experience the highs and lows of life that others with a different blend are incapable of doing.

KING DAVID

David, the ancient King of Israel, was a Sanguine-Melancholy. His life was a roller coaster of emotional highs and lows. He wrote many psalms that record the expression of his deep emotions. David left us some of the most inspiring and beautiful poetry ever written.

WHAT CAN HAPPEN

Without self-awareness and self-control, it is easy to see how the Sanguine-Melancholy thoughts and emotions can control their behavior. If they allow their thoughts to go unmanaged, they will bounce off the walls of their mind causing confusion and frustration.

Some have told me that because they did not manage their thoughts well that they jumped to conclusions and convinced themselves that something was true when it was not. If they allow their emotions to be freely expressed, they will overreact to most anything that happens.

SUDDEN OUTBURST

Anyone can have a sudden outburst of emotion out of anger or a need for self-protection. The Sanguine-Melancholy is capable of a sudden burst of emotion for a variety of reasons including being embarrassed, being rejected, failing, etc.

There is another possibility. As mentioned earlier, when the blend of the Sanguine-Melancholy temperament is followed by the Choleric (D) as a third temperament, then a sudden display of assertiveness or bluntness is common and frequent. This not only surprises the one on the receiving end of the sudden bluntness, but also the one delivering the message. The Sanguine-Melancholy that has Phlegmatic as their third (which is most common) produces a softer expression of this blend. They are capable of having a sudden outburst of emotions as well, but it is far less frequent, if at all.

If you think that the Choleric (D) is your third temperament then be aware that there is always a possibility of an unexpected, abrupt response. Consciously guard yourself from allowing abrupt comments to be made. When you feel it coming on, make a choice to not be abrupt and blunt. It will take some time to gain control over this tendency because it happens so quickly, but keep working on it and you will eventually eliminate it from your behavior. When you do, you will be much more effective when making your point.

WHAT CAN YOU DO?

The Sanguine-Melancholy temperament is the most versatile, gifted, and creative of all the temperament blends. As a Sanguine-Melancholy you know that your strong emotions make it difficult for you at times to control yourself. When your natural strengths are used and your natural weaknesses are controlled, you are capable of achieving most anything that you set your mind to doing. Here are some things that you can do to maximize your potential and eliminate the negative impact that your thoughts and emotions may be having on your life.

BE AWARE

Be aware that you are naturally capable of thinking more quickly and feeling more deeply than any of the other temperament blends. This combination means that you have a wide range of capabilities and creative potential.

TAKE CONTROL

Self-control is the most important characteristic in the growth process. Self-control can be defined as the ability to exercise restraint or control over your mind (thoughts), emotions (feelings), and will (behavior). Proverbs 25:28 is clear about what can happen when one fails to control themselves; "He that has no rule over his own spirit is like a city which is broken down and without walls." Without self-control no one has defenses against their own thoughts, feelings, and behavior.

Proverbs 16:32 states, "He who is slow to anger is better than the mighty, And he who rules his spirit, than he who captures a city." It is better to be slow to anger than it is to be exceedingly strong. If you were very strong you would still fall short of the one who has learned self-control! This proverb is contrasting self-control with physical strength. Some spend more time in the gym getting physically fit than they do learning to control their thoughts and emotions. The greatest power is self-control, not physical strength.

USE "THOUGHT STOPPING"

Not stopping the flood of thoughts will result in a lifestyle habit of allowing your thoughts to run rampant and your emotions to be freely expressed. One technique to help you control your thoughts and emotions is called "thought stopping." The idea is that you issue the command "Stop!" when you experience too many thoughts at once.

Calling *time out* gives you time to decide to either pursue one of the thoughts or think about something entirely different. Repeatedly using the "stop" command every time you are flooded with thoughts will enable you to be in control not only of your thoughts, but also of your emotions. If at times you release strong, negative emotions it is because you believe it is ok to do so. Once you decide that it is not ok, you will stop. Your thoughts therefore will control your emotions.

Once you have "stopped" the flood of thoughts, decide to operate on facts, not on speculation or what you think is true. Do not allow thoughts that are not based on objective truth to linger. Do not speculate or guess. By being factual, you will save yourself time and frustration. Decide to control your thoughts so your thoughts and emotions will not control you.

Not every Sanguine-Melancholy will have difficulty controlling their thoughts and emotions as discussed in this chapter. This is because not every Sanguine-Melancholy will have the same level of intensity. It's the intensity presence of these two opposite and opposing temperaments that gives an individual the greatest challenge of self-control. Remember, intensity levels vary from mild, to moderate, to extreme. So the more intense the temperament, the more difficult it is to control it's expression. Because of this, some need to work harder than others to control their thoughts and emotions.

10

CONTROL YOUR MOODS

 *I travel light. I think the most important thing is to be in a good mood and enjoy life, wherever you are.*

-DIANE VON FURSTENBERG | FASHION DESIGNER

CONTROL YOUR MOODS

The Sanguine-Melancholy may have a noticeable shift in their normal mood state at times. There are several possible reasons for this to occur.

NOT ENOUGH ALONE TIME

The Sanguine-Melancholy has an extroverted and introverted temperament blend. This is a unique blend of opposite and opposing tendencies that produce creative potential and internal tension.

The Sanguine part of the temperament blend drives the person to being active, being with people, being spontaneous, and having fun. The Melancholy part of the temperament blend drives the person to collect information, to be alone, to analyze the information, and to develop a plan. Because both want to be in control of the person (often at the same time) these two opposite temperaments are at war with each other. When these two opposite and opposing drives are not understood, controlled, and directed, tension, confusion, and anxiety occurs, which produces a noticeable change in mood.

Sometimes the Sanguine-Melancholy may give too much time to being with people. They may go for days or weeks without a significant break from activity with others. Their usual sleep patterns will likely be interrupted as well. In so doing, they neglect their natural need to be alone which will cause stress, irritability, and a noticeable shift in their mood.

FAILURE TO HAVE A PLAN

The need of the Melancholy part of this blend demands a daily plan in which to operate. Without such a plan, a Sanguine-Melancholy cannot and will not function effectively. The Melancholy side of this blend needs to know what, when, where, and how something will be done. Without this need being met, the Melancholy part cannot be sure that they are doing the right thing so they are hesitant to do anything. Without a plan in place, the Sanguine part is not relaxed or comfortable either because they are concerned that they will make a mistake and look less than favorable in the eyes of others. Moodiness will occur until there is a detailed plan in place on which to operate.

BEING EMBARRASSED

If the Sanguine-Melancholy is discredited or disrespected in any way, it can cause them to immediately withdraw from others. Image is very important so when embarrassment happens there is usually a noticeable shift in mood because of the emotional pain experienced.

BEING REJECTED

The pain the Sanguine-Melancholy experiences when rejected is felt at their deepest level. When this occurs they can change from being friendly and talkative to not speaking to anyone. The change in mood can be sudden. They may become sarcastic, rude, demeaning, aggressive, and even argumentative.

Gary Fusco, Ph.D., told me about a Sanguine-Melancholy wife that exploded on her husband just after he came in from work. She had fixed him soup and it was still simmering in the container on the stove. Her plan was to have a nice dinner around a well decorated table. He was surprised, delighted, and eager, so he walked over and tasted it with a spoon right out of the pot. She erupted with an enormous display of emotion, screaming and saying harmful things to him and about him. To say that he was stunned is an understatement. Several days later with the help of Dr. Fusco they were able to determine that she had taken her husband's actions as disrespect and rejection. She expected him to be courteous and wait for the table to be prepared so they could enjoy the meal together. She said that he had ruined the moment even though he thought he was showing approval by wanting to taste the soup immediately.

The behavior of the Sanguine-Melancholy who lacks self-awareness and self-control can move quickly from one emotional state to another. At the bottom of their swing may be depression. Depression is the result of being stuck and not moving beyond a disappointing event.

WHAT CAN YOU DO?

BE AWARE

Be aware that it is normal and natural for mood shifts to occur with the Sanguine-Melancholy temperament blend. If you are unsure that this represents your behavior, ask your mate or a person you trust if they have noticed mood shifts.

TAKE CONTROL

Accept ownership that this is your behavior and decide to take control of your natural tendencies to prevent noticeable shifts in your mood state from occurring.

If you address the four main areas mentioned in this chapter, you will gain control over what causes the shifts in mood. Make sure you have enough alone time every day so you can review the day and plan for tomorrow. Remember that it is okay to just want to be alone.

Actively seek effective coping skills to deal with being embarrassed and being rejected. Apply the suggestions made in this book and the shifts in your mood will be greatly minimized or eliminated.

11

DO NOT BE CONCERNED ABOUT YOUR IMAGE

DO NOT BE CONCERNED ABOUT YOUR IMAGE

Since the Sanguine-Melancholy tends to struggle with the fear of being rejected, it is natural that protecting their image can be very important to them. When image is too important, then anything that discredits them can ignite a strong emotional reaction. The event doesn't have to be real--just their *perception* of the event. It doesn't have to be much either, just a concerned look, a word spoken, or a sharp tone of voice can become triggers. When image is too important and there is a lack of self-control, emotions may erupt with yelling, screaming and harsh words--shocking anyone on the receiving end. In the following sections, we will go over what it looks like to be too concerned about your image.

SELF-CENTERED

A self-centered person thinks mostly of themselves and how they are being perceived by others. Significant thought is given to how to make a good impression with what they say or how they dress. They are centered on what they want, what is best for them, and what makes them happy to the exclusion of the needs of others.

Ted is an example of one who is too concerned about his image. Ted had been married to Mary for seventeen years, had a good job with a comfortable income and was considered by those who knew him to be a productive and likable person. As a husband however, he was rude, demeaning, and controlling. He kept his money separate from hers. He bought toys for himself--expensive toys. He even took his own vacations leaving his wife home alone.

One evening Ted and Mary went out to eat and to discuss their diminished relationship. As had happened so often in the past, their discussion soon became an argument and once again he was in verbal attack mode. Finally, she just couldn't take it anymore and stood up to leave. With rage in his eyes, gritting his teeth, he said to her, "Don't you dare leave and embarrass me!" It was clear that Ted was more concerned about his image than his wife.

When Mary married Ted she thought she had married a teddy bear, but to her dismay, she discovered that Ted was a bear all right, a bear to live with. Such a person is not only self-centered but also self-absorbed.

One person who fits this profile went so far as to divorce his wife because she reported physical abuse to his military commanding officer. It was true. He then tried to win her back. He told her that if she would tell his commanding officer that she lied about the abuse that he would marry her again. All he was concerned about was himself and his image before his commanding officer--not his wife.

Those married to a self-centered Sanguine-Melancholy tell me they often walk on eggshells--not knowing when the next explosion may occur. One Sanguine-Melancholy wife threw her husband out of the house for an insignificant event because it embarrassed her in front of his parents. It was never resolved and they divorced.

ATTENTION SEEKING

Some who are Sanguine-Melancholy may be so image driven that much of what they do is designed to draw attention to themselves. They accomplish this in a variety of ways including what they wear (or don't wear) or their behavior. Males will sometimes wear heavily starched shirts to set themselves apart. Both male and females have the unique ability to put together well coordinated outfits that are eye-catchers. All of this may be done to draw attention to themselves, mark their individuality, and cause them to be noticed by others.

While doing consulting work in Atlanta, Georgia I interviewed a young lady who made up as perfectly as anyone I had ever seen. Her makeup, hair, and clothes were all perfectly coordinated. She had spent hours putting it all together and looked ready for a professional photo shoot. At an appropriate moment in the conversation I commented on this and she said, "Even if I am ill I will get out of bed and fix my hair and makeup and then get back into bed. I will not let anyone see me less than this!"

If clothing does not get attention, then they will do it with their behavior. This will range anywhere from withdrawing when they are not the center of attention, to running away, to keeping things stirred up in the family or at work. Some will do whatever it takes to be the center of attention--positive or negative. There is a saying in Hollywood that sums up their approach, "There is no such thing as bad press."

SELF-PROMOTING

Image can be so important to some that if attention is not freely given they will actively seek recognition. If others do not lavish them with praise they will do it themselves. They will become their own press agent! I heard a so-called motivational speaker who liked to brag about all that he had accomplished, how wonderful he was, and how good he was in a certain sport. There was nothing inspirational about his presentation because all he did was make it clear that he was a special man with great talent.

When I was in college, we would have guest speakers come three times a week. One speaker who came often never failed to point out his great achievements. Once he held up a newspaper containing a large article about himself showing the audience what a wonderful person he was! While he was a good speaker with a great message, students were turned off by him and unfortunately, to his message as well. It's a shame to see the messenger get in the way of the message.

NEED TO BE IMPORTANT

The importance of image can be so strong in the Sanguine-Melancholy that they project the appearance of being important even when they have not yet accomplished anything significant. Some will do most anything to appear important or at least be recognized for something. Once recognized, it may go to their head; I call this the Muhammad Ali Syndrome, "I'm the Greatest!"

A young man who fit this profile went to college to become an accountant. He said that he did not care about the degree or even becoming an accountant, he just wanted his name on the door of his father's company.

The story is told of what Marlene Dietrich (an award winning actress) did while attending a 1962 Christmas party in Switzerland. She was one of the many star-studded guests. She was sitting in the corner looking bored since no one was paying her any attention. She suddenly left the room and a short time later came back with some records. She got everyone's attention and said, "Here, you must play this. These are my applauses." She had records of her applauses, no music on them, just applauses!

Of course, not every Sanguine-Melancholy will push their need to be important to this extreme, but it does happen. To appear important, many will pursue marvelous dreams and grandiose schemes to the exclusion of what is really important. In their mind it's always just around the corner or over the next hill. If something happens to their dream, they may say, as one thirty-year-old male said, "I almost made it big but didn't because others did not want to see me successful."

SENSITIVE

The Sanguine-Melancholy can be so concerned about their image that they can be very sensitive about how they are treated and what others think about them. "Do they like me?" "How am I doing?" "Did I say the right thing?" "How does my hair look?" These are the kinds of thoughts that often go rushing through their mind when with someone--especially one they've just met. If they feel uncomfortable with others, they will usually act more formal or withdraw by being cautious and guarded.

They can be extremely nice or aloof to compensate for the concern about their image. Their behavior can be so unpredictable that it causes others to be tense. Others never know what to expect so they are unable to let their guard down and relax around them fearing that they may get upset.

Image can be so important to the Sanguine-Melancholy that if they are laughed at, made fun of, mocked, or disrespected in anyway they are capable of exploding with emotion or withdrawing.

IMAGE CONCERNS AT WORK

The Sanguine-Melancholy is able to get great positions because of their wide range of abilities. Once on the job they learn quickly and get promoted by performing better than everyone else.

IN SALES

I was a consultant for seven years with a national company that had offices in every state. Every month for six years I taught their new salespeople how to sell using the temperament model of behavior. During that time the best students were Sanguine-Melancholy. They comprehended the product's selling points quickly and "role-played" perfectly. They astounded everyone with their ability and convinced management that they would excel in sales as soon as they were in the field. Once in the field, the result was the opposite--they had the greatest fail rate. The problem was they gave in to their fear of rejection and it kept them from contacting prospects to sell the product. Most failed within the first month and many times they quit the first day out of training school.

The irony was that when a Sanguine-Melancholy decided that it was more painful to fail than to be rejected by a prospect, they were the best salesperson the company hired! They were the ones who set and broke all of the sales records.

IN MANAGEMENT

The Sanguine-Melancholy is very capable and their abilities are usually recognized so they rise into middle and upper management level positions quickly.

There is, however, a caution to be noted. In The Peter Principle, Laurence J. Peter explains that people are promoted to their highest level of incompetence. That is what often happens with the immature Sanguine-Melancholy. To them, the issue is not being an *effective* manager, the issue is *being* the manager. Having a title is usually their goal.

An immature Sanguine-Melancholy can be so driven to be important that the end justifies the means, and they have a double standard. The result is that in a management position they may treat people that are equal to or above them with one standard and those they consider beneath them with another. They can be charming to their superiors leading them to believe this is the way they are all the time with everyone. They are polite, helpful, and always wanting to please their superiors. To those they perceive are beneath them, the immature Sanguine-Melancholy can be pushy, unreasonable, and controlling. The immature Sanguine-Melancholy may push those under their leadership to produce so they will look competent in the eyes of their superiors. Those in management over the Sanguine-Melancholy will not see how the manager is treating others--they only see how they are being treated.

One very nice lady worked in the cosmetic department of a large upscale store for several years under an immature Sanguine-Melancholy manager. When she began working in that store, there were about forty ladies in different cosmetic lines. Within less than a year, the turnover was so great that only four of the original staff remained. Virtually everyone left because of the way they had been treated by that manager.

WHAT CAN YOU DO?

BE AWARE

Be aware that you can place too much importance on protecting your image. To increase your self-awareness, be objective and investigate why you think protecting your image is so important. Seriously consider the reasons discussed in this chapter.

If you are doing things to draw attention to yourself, to project an image of importance, then realize that such behavior is self-serving and others are likely to have a negative opinion of you.

TAKE CONTROL

Accept ownership if this is your behavior and decide to stop trying to look important and concentrate on doing something important that will benefit other people. The most contented and fulfilled people I know are committed to something bigger than themselves.

AS A MANAGER

If you are a manager, treat people the way you want to be treated. Treat people with the dignity and respect that you desire and always be gracious in your responses. A manager is responsible to model behavior that is to be followed.

MOTIVE?

Why are you doing the things that you do? Is it to draw attention to yourself? Is it to make you look important? Do you want to be the center of attention?

The wisdom to not draw attention to yourself has been around for at least 3,000 years. Proverbs 27: 2 says, *"Don't praise yourself. Let someone else do it. Let the praise come from a stranger and not from your own mouth."* Bruce Waltke (2004) writes in The Book of Proverbs, "...it can be inferred that self-praise is unfitting because it destroys one's relationship with God and with people. The Lord detests the proud, and society dislikes and discounts the boaster. Instead of exalting the boaster, self-praise diminishes one's status and suggests that one is proud, feels undervalued, and is socially insecure. The admonition protects one against self-deception and flattery." A German proverb says, "Self-praise stinks, a friend's praise limps, a stranger's praise rings."

When you seek the limelight and want to be important, it questions the motive on which you operate. Other people do notice. Do what you do because it is the right thing to do. Chuck Swindoll is a pastor and author of many helpful Christian books. He said that he has a sign on his desk that is carved out of wood and states simply... *"What's My Motive?"*

12

CONTROL YOUR NEED TO TALK

 *There is a difference between listening and waiting for your turn to speak.*

-SIMON SINEK | AUTHOR

CONTROL YOUR NEED TO TALK

The Sanguine-Melancholy may at times talk excessively. There are several possible explanations.

ISOLATION

The Sanguine-Melancholy routinely needs to be with, by, or around people. If there are reasons beyond the control of the Sanguine-Melancholy that this need has not been met, they may overwhelm others when the opportunity presents itself. If the Sanguine-Melancholy has chosen to isolate themselves, the same result may occur when they are finally able to talk to someone. They can be so excited to be around people that they dominate the conversation.

One lady told me that she and her husband routinely get into arguments because she talks excessively when they have guests in their home. She explained that she stays home each day and does not have much contact with people. When guests are invited over, she overwhelms them! When we discussed her Sanguine-Melancholy temperament, she realized the reason she was talking too much when guests were in her home was because she had not been around people all day and was excited to talk to someone!

SELF-DEFENSE

If a Sanguine-Melancholy is being confronted about their behavior, they may talk excessively to prevent the other person from presenting their case. They can get so intense when defending themselves that they ignore what other people are saying and even talk over them. They are usually trying to use up all the time to avoid being exposed.

CENTER OF ATTENTION

Sometimes the Sanguine-Melancholy will talk excessively just to be the center of attention. What better way to be the center of attention than to talk louder and more often than anyone else. The Sanguine-Melancholy is a great story teller and can mesmerize an audience with passion and intrigue.

WHAT CAN YOU DO?

BE AWARE

Be aware that you may talk excessively at times. Be objective and consider the reasons mentioned in this chapter. Be aware that others notice when someone dominates the conversation because they feel left out.

TAKE CONTROL

Take ownership that this is your behavior and decide to control your need to talk too much. Develop the art of active listening.

13

BE CREATIVE

BE CREATIVE

The creativity of the Sanguine and Melancholy is seen in art, music, writing, design, decorating, architecture, computer programming, cooking, etc. They can be creative in writing songs, singing songs, playing a musical instrument, acting, painting works of art, writing poetry, and excelling in sports. Some are great at problem solving. History is filled with the great works of these gifted and creative people.

Creativity can be seen in other temperament blends as well. For example our granddaughter, Danielle, who is a Melancholy-Sanguine (C/I) is a gifted photographer. She started a wedding photography business while still in high-school.

Some creative people do not develop their abilities for various reasons. I spoke with one Sanguine-Melancholy lady who had a dominating husband and decided that she did not have much to offer with her life. Once she understood her creative potential, she gained confidence to explore her interest in decorating. To her amazement, she discovered that she was very good at putting colors together, arranging furniture, and decorating her home. She was very surprised at the number of compliments she received from family and friends.

Others do not express their creativity consistently because they fear their creative work will not be well received. Fear overwhelms them and they find a reason to do something else. Charles Baudouin, a French-swiss Psychoanalyst said, "No matter how hard you work for success, if your thoughts are saturated with the fear of failure, it will kill your efforts, neutralize your endeavors and make success impossible."

Consider Thomas Edison's story. His teachers said he was not smart enough to learn anything. He was fired from his first two jobs he had for being unproductive. As an inventor he made at least 10,000 unsuccessful attempts at inventing a long lasting filament for the light bulb. When a reporter asked, "How did it feel to fail 10,000 times?" Edison replied, "I didn't fail 10,000 times. The light bulb was an invention with 10,000 steps."

Sometimes it is not so much the fear of failure that gets in the way, it could simply be boredom. The Sanguine-Melancholy will at times start a project only to get bored and abandon the idea to chase another bigger and better dream. This could be just as debilitating as the fear of failure because once unchecked, they may find themselves unable to see anything to completion.

WHAT CAN YOU DO?

BE AWARE

Be aware that you have the natural ability to be creative in things like art, music, decorating, problem solving, etc.

TAKE CONTROL

Do not neglect your creative potential. Pursue your interest and allow your creativity to express itself.

BE CONSISTENT

Pursue your creative interest and be consistent. It does not matter what other people may think about your creative abilities or work. What's important is that you express this vital part of your temperament blend. You will find it rewarding and satisfying.

14

BE A GOOD COACH

At the end of the day, you're responsible for yourself and your actions and that's all you can control. So rather than be frustrated with what you can't control, try to fix the things you can.

-KEVIN GARNETT | PRO BASKETBALL PLAYER

BE A GOOD COACH

In order to move toward maximizing your potential and having a more productive and fulfilling life, become a good coach of your natural tendencies.

As a Sanguine-Melancholy, imagine that there are three people in your head: there is *you*, the Sanguine part, and the Melancholy part. The Sanguine and Melancholy are urges within you wanting to have their needs met. The Sanguine wants to be with people and have fun whereas the Melancholy wants to be alone to think and plan. These two opposite and opposing urges compete for *your* attention and cause you anxiety when they do not get what they need. Now that you know the names of these two urges within, you are in a position to not only understand their needs, but to choose when they can have their needs met.

As the coach, be aware that your Sanguine part has a strong tendency to want to be with people and may have *too much* fun on occasion to the neglect of your Melancholy part. The Melancholy urge to be alone can hit you when you are with people, causing a slight shift in your mood. As the coach, remind yourself that the Melancholy urge is wanting to pull you away and that it will happen soon. With this awareness, the typical anxiety that normally follows an episode like this will be greatly lessened.

BEING A COACH
FIGURE 3

SANGUINE	COACH	MELANCHOLY
People	*take control*	*Privacy*
Active		*Think*
Fun		*Plan*

BE AWARE

Realize that you can control your urges to be with people and to be alone. You are the coach, so you decide when to express your temperament needs and do not allow your temperament tendencies to control you.

TAKE CONTROL

Realize that through self-coaching you can develop better self-control over your natural tendencies.

15

USE POSITIVE SELF-TALK & VISUALIZE SUCCESS

USE POSITIVE SELF-TALK & VISUALIZE SUCCESS

The way the brain functions is we talk to ourselves and we see pictures. We do not actually "hear" a voice when we talk to ourselves but everyone does "self-talk." The key to self-talk is to be sure that you are saying the right things to yourself.

If you want to gain more control of your emotions, fears, and anxieties, use positive self-talk and see yourself being in control of your emotions, fears, and anxieties in a difficult situation. Visualize your success and how you are going to respond in advance.

Once you think about it, you may discover just how much negative self-talk you may be doing. Many say things like, "I can't do that," or "I may fail if I try that." If you were to change your self-talk to, "I can do that," and "If I fail, I'll try again," you will be putting yourself in the best possible position to be successful at whatever endeavor you choose.

We also "see" pictures in our mind. For example, if I were to ask you to tell me about the most tasty meal you can remember, you would actually "see" the meal in your "mind's eye." If you were to describe the place where you live, you would actually "see" your home in your "mind's eye" as you described it to me.

I was introduced to the concept of visualizing positive images when I read Psycho-Cybernetics (1960) by Maxwell Maltz in 1979. Here are excerpts of Michael C. Gray's review of the book (2001):

> Psycho-Cybernetics is a classic personal development book. Most of the current speakers in the area of personal development, including Zig Ziglar, Tony Robbins, Brian Tracy and others owe a debt to Maxwell Maltz for the foundation of their material. The psychological training of Olympic athletes is also based on the concepts in Psycho-Cybernetics.
>
> Maxwell Maltz was a cosmetic surgeon. He was amazed when, after he had performed some impressive reconstruction procedures, patients would complain they couldn't see the difference! "I still feel ugly."
>
> Maltz recognized that, in addition to the reconstruction work on

the outside, the patient needed to have reconstruction work on the "inside," on the patient's self-image.

The self image is a mental picture that each person has of himself or herself. It includes our beliefs about our abilities and deficiencies, whether we are popular or not, and so forth. Some of these beliefs may have been true at one time, but are no longer true. Until those beliefs are changed, our behavior will continue to be defined by those beliefs. For example, a person may have had a traumatic automobile accident when he or she was driving. He or she may be afraid to drive because of the self-image as a "bad driver." Until that self-image is changed, that person will continue to be limited by that belief.

Maltz saw human behavior as a negative feedback (cybernetic) system. This is the type of system used in a torpedo or a guided missile. When the torpedo or missile is fired, it will correct its course to reach its goal. People also correct their behavior to reach their goals, including behaving according to their self image.

One of Maltz's key concepts was the Theater of the Mind, or synthetic experience. Here is an example of how it works. There are three teams of basketball players. One team practices making free throws. The second team doesn't practice. The third team sits on a bench and mentally practices making free throws. When the three teams are tested, the team that practiced out-scores the team that didn't practice. However, the team that mentally practiced performs nearly as well as the team that actually practiced.

Maltz found he could actually improve performance by helping an individual mentally "see" himself or herself doing the activity perfectly. Thousands, possibly millions, of people have benefited by putting these ideas to work.

I was convinced this concept was true because of an experience I had while I was in graduate school before I read the book by Maxwell Maltz. Most everyone lives on a tight budget when in graduate school and I was no exception. I put lots of miles on my car and it was in need of an overhaul. I did not have the money to pay someone to overhaul the engine so I decided to do it myself.

I had two weeks off in-between classes that summer when I planned to overhaul the engine. Two months before doing the work, I studied the motor manual that had diagrams of the engine showing the smallest detail in how the motor had been assembled. I visualized actually taking the motor apart, piece by piece. I labeled cans to put bolts in that I had removed so I would know where to put them when I re-assembled the engine. I actually overhauled the engine in every detail in my mind's eye a dozen times.

Now came reality. It took a week and a half to complete the project and when I started the engine for the first time, it ran as bad as it did before the overhaul. That's right, no improvement! I visualized success and now that it wasn't happening, I had to use positive self-talk!

I called my friend Richard who was a master mechanic to get some emergency help. He said it sounded like a valve was stuck and I may have to tear the engine apart again. Not good news! Then he told me the problem could be fixed with a piece of wood and a hammer. All this time I had used precision tools to overhaul the engine and the solution was a piece of wood and hammer? I had to use more positive self-talk trusting that he was right.

I followed his instructions using the new "precision tools" to hit the uncooperative valve stem while the engine was running (those who know about engines know what all this means). It took three very powerful direct hits to the piece of wood that was resting on the stubborn valve stem to make it work. As soon as the valve started doing what it was supposed to do, the engine ran as smooth as a new one. The engine overhaul was successful because I had visualized doing it in my mind's eye well in advance and used positive self-talk when it wasn't going as planned.

Three months after successfully accomplishing this great feat, I was rear-ended and the car was totaled! Such is life!

Despite the fact that my success still ended up in a wreck, the experience revealed that Psycho-Cybernetics does work. This concept awakened my awareness to the process of what can happen when you visualize success in advance of what you want to accomplish.

WHAT CAN YOU DO?

BE AWARE

Be aware that you may not be seeing yourself as being in control of your thoughts, emotions, and behavior. Become aware of how you can see yourself succeeding in life. Become aware of the nature of your self-talk. Is it positive or negative?

TAKE CONTROL

Decide to take control of your self-talk and what you are visualizing. Decide to eliminate the negative self-talk and see yourself as being successful controlling your thoughts, emotions, and behavior, by focusing on a positive, successful outcome.

PLAN

Use your alone time to rehearse positive self-talk and to visualize success in every area of your life. Clean up your self-talk and be sure you say only positive things to yourself. Take the time to see yourself as being successful--controlling your emotional reactions, fears, and anxieties.

UNDERSTAND THE THINKING PROCESS

Behavior is caused by your response to what you believe to be true. Your normal, daily activity is based on certain beliefs; what you say, where you go, what you eat, what you do for entertainment, etc. An exception to this is the automatic response of "fight or flight" which occurs in an emergency.

1. Your beliefs cause self-talk.
If the belief or emotion is negative, your self-talk will be negative. If your belief or emotion is positive. the self-talk will be positive.

2. Your self-talk determines your attitude.
An attitude is an opinion or perspective representing part of your belief system and is usually a habitual way of thinking. Attitudes are either positive or negative. If your self-talk is positive, your attitude will be positive. If your self-talk is negative, your attitude will be negative.

3. Attitudes determine your emotions.
Emotions are either pleasant, such as love, joy, and happiness, or unpleasant, such as anger, fear, and anxiety.

4. Emotions influence your behavior.
Behavior is observable activity, conduct or style. We either involve ourselves in the task/goal or avoid the task/goal.

5. Behavior produces results.
Results can be productive or nonproductive.
Self-talk, attitudes, emotions, behavior and results are all manifestations of

your belief system which is represented by your self-talk. When trying to control, modify or change your own behavior, remember these are all surface expressions that represent a certain, identifiable belief.

To change your behavior, change your self-talk. Instead of repeating self-defeating, negative self-talk, say only positive, encouraging things to yourself. See figure 4 below.

THE THINKING PROCESS
FIGURE 4

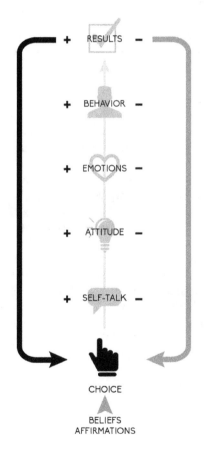

To change your behavior, change your self-talk from being negative to being positive. For example, change your self-talk from "I can't do this" to "I can do this;" from "I feel rejected" to "I do not take being rejected personally;" from "I'm bad because I failed" to "I'm ok, failure is part of life, I'll try again." Identify your negative self-talk, stop saying it to yourself, and replace it with positive self-talk.

I'm a pro-football fan and I have a favorite team that I have painfully followed for more years than I care to remember. I have watched touchdowns scored by the hundreds by my team. Many times the running back will score and then go into all kinds of gyrations. They strut, flip, dance, and jump into the stands. I've wondered aloud, "How much time do they practice doing all that stuff?"

Jim Brown never did any of those things. He is perhaps the greatest of all running backs to play in the National Football League. In an interview many years ago he was asked why he did not celebrate when he scored a touchdown. His answer was simple, "I expected to score." He was not surprised because he saw himself scoring touchdowns. That's why he scored! He planned ahead to score touchdowns.

Many years ago Walt Disney developed the concept of Disney World but he died before it was completed. The story is told that while the executives were looking over the completed project, one of them said, "It's a shame that Walt was not here to see this." One of the others remarked, "He did see it, that's why it's here."

My brother Mike comments in his unpublished notes on what the writer of Psalms 42:5-6 did when he felt depressed;

> This Psalm describes discouragement as the soul being cast down. In that state of mind, the Psalmist did several things: He talked to himself. "Why are you cast down, O my soul? And why are you disquieted within me?' He thought about the Lord. "O my God, my soul is cast down within me; therefore I will remember You from the land of the Jordan, and from the heights of Hermon, from the Hill Mizar." He sought the Lord. "As the deer pants for the water brooks, so pants my soul for You, O God" (Ps. 42:1). He put his confidence in the Lord (Ps. 42:5, 11,). He praised the Lord (Ps. 42:5, 11)."

When you are depressed, do what the Psalmist did and see how quickly you feel encouraged.

GET MOTIVATED

Many years ago the mother of a nineteen year old boy asked me why her son was so lazy. She explained that her son lays on the couch every day for hours at a time and was not trying to find a job. She said with frustration, "The boy is just not motivated, what can I do?" I said to her, "I'm sorry to be the one to tell you this, but your son is highly motivated...to lay on the couch!"

The goal of the young man mentioned above was to lay on the couch. If that were not his goal he would do something else. All behavior is goal directed so if you want to change your behavior, you have to set a goal to be different. Once you set a goal, there are three things that must be involved in order for you to be motivated: mind, emotion, and will.

My wife and I visited a Firehouse Subs restaurant and ordered a sandwich. The employee asked us, "Did we want it fully involved?" Puzzled, I ask, "What does that mean?" He quickly elaborated--do we want everything on the sandwich? I responded, "Of course, put everything you have in it!" To be motivated, you have to put everything you have into it; your mind, emotion, and will. To achieve your goal, the following must merge together as one.

Will
First, you must exercise your will and decide to change a particular behavior. What do you want to change? Clearly state your desired change as a goal in one sentence. For example, "I choose to overcome my fear of rejection."

Mind
Second, you must engage your mind by thinking of positive ways of achieving your goal of overcoming your fear of being rejected. Think about how you can overcome your fear, have positive self-talk and picture yourself accomplishing your goal.

Emotion
Third, get excited about achieving your goal. See yourself as unconcerned about being rejected and imagine the feelings you would like to experience.

If you want to change, you will; people do what they want to do. State your goal clearly, decide to change, see yourself being different, and get excited about overcoming your fear...and you will!

16

MAKE HEALTHY CHOICES

 *We either make ourselves miserable or we make ourselves strong. The amount of work is the same.*

-CARLOS CASTENADA | AUTHOR

MAKE HEALTHY CHOICES

Maximize your potential by making good choices for your life in the areas mentioned in this book. Have a healthy balance between spending time with people and spending time alone. Set aside enough daily time to develop a plan for the next day. Develop effective coping skills to deal with your fears. Control your thoughts and emotions. Do not take things personally. Decide to be consistent and follow-through on projects. Pursue your creativity in a healthy manner. Become a better coach of your natural temperament tendencies. Visualize being successful doing these things mentioned above.

CHOICES TO MAKE

Overcoming a particular issue that has an unhealthy control over you begins with a choice. A professor I had in graduate school, Dr. Howard Hendricks, said many times, *"It's not where you are in life that is important, it's the direction in which you are traveling."* Once you decide to overcome an issue that keeps you derailed, you will change the direction in which your life is going. The following is a check list of the all areas to address to maximize your potential that this book has mentioned. Look over the list and make your healthy decisions so you can live your full potential.

- ☐ I choose to balance my need to be with people and my need to be alone
- ☐ I choose to have a daily plan
- ☐ I choose to develop the necessary coping skills to deal with my fears, especially the fear of being rejected
- ☐ I choose to control my thoughts and emotions
- ☐ I choose to not take things personally
- ☐ I choose to be consistent
- ☐ I choose to use my creativity productively
- ☐ I choose to become a better coach of my natural tendencies
- ☐ I choose to visualize success
- ☐ I choose to make good choices

CONSIDER THIS

You are right now the person you want to be. No one else has made the choices that caused you to be who you are at this very moment. You made those choices so you cannot blame anyone or any event for the person you have become. You alone are responsible for who you are. The question is: do you want to continue being who you have become? If the answer is no, then what kind of person do you want to be?

The truth is that you will not do anything that you do not want to do. If you like the person you have become then continue doing what you have been doing. If, however, you want something different in one or more areas of your life then you must make some changes. You cannot keep doing what you've been doing and expect different results.

WHAT CAN YOU DO?

BE AWARE

Be aware that the choices you have made formed you into the person you are today. Be aware that you can change anything you want to by making a choice to do so.

TAKE CONTROL

Take ownership that this is the behavior you want and decide to take control of the choices you are making.

17

HAVE A POSITIVE IMPACT

HAVE A POSITIVE IMPACT

To be Sanguine means that you easily and naturally have a positive impact on others. When you are with others and you are in your Sanguine mode, people naturally feel better about themselves and even get excited. When in your Sanguine mode, you are friendly and winsome and have a positive influence on other people.

Tim LaHaye in *Your Temperament: Discover Its Potential* (1984) says, "Sparky Sanguine is a warm, buoyant, lively, and 'enjoying' person. Mr. Sanguine has an unusual capacity for enjoying himself and usually passes on his fun-loving spirit. The moment he enters a room he tends to lift the spirits of everyone present by his exuberant conversation."

When you are in your Melancholy mode, your positive impact on others is because of detailed explanations logically given. The command of specific details and the winsomeness of the Sanguine combines to make a fantastic story teller. The way you tell a story captures people's imaginations and enables them to re-live the experience with you.

You will have the most positive impact on others when you are exercising self-control and you are operating out of the strengths of your Sanguine-Melancholy temperament.

The Book of Proverbs recognizes the importance of being upbeat and positive. Notice the following:

•Proverbs 15:13 "A glad heart makes a cheerful face, but by sorrow of heart the spirit is crushed."

•Proverbs 15:15 "Every day is hard for those who suffer, but a happy heart is like a continual feast."

•Proverbs 17:22 "A cheerful heart is good medicine, but a broken spirit saps a person's strength."

WHAT CAN YOU DO?

BE AWARE

Be aware that as a Sanguine-Melancholy, you have a positive impact on people in two ways. First, your Sanguine naturally causes others to feel better about themselves when you are around. You do not have to do anything special just show up! Second, be aware that when you express your Melancholy side to others they feel better because you have given them detailed information.

TAKE CONTROL

Take ownership that this is your behavior and decide to have a positive impact on others. Be yourself as described above and it will happen naturally.

Have a positive impact on others with your winsome, creative abilities. When you do, people will feel better about themselves and so will you! Everyone loves a Sanguine!

 *"Be yourself, everyone else is taken"*

-OSCAR WILDE

18

GET A GOOD NIGHT'S SLEEP

Give it to God and go to sleep.

-ANONYMOUS

GET A GOOD NIGHT'S SLEEP

As a Sanguine-Melancholy, you know all too well how difficult it is to get to sleep and stay asleep! Routinely I am told by Sanguine-Melancholies that they get between four to six hours of sleep a night and they even wake up several times during the night.

Many have told me that they were convinced that something was wrong with their brain so they sought medication to help them sleep. A lot of times even that did not help. There are reasons for this and it has nothing to do with a defective brain or the need for sleep-aid medication.

NOT ENOUGH ALONE TIME

If you are not getting enough alone time during the day to process your thoughts, then you may be using your going-to-sleep-time to catch up. While you are trying to go to sleep, you will review the day and plan for tomorrow.

HAVING A CREATIVE MOMENT

When a creative moment hits, your brain will not let you relax. You're thinking about what to do, how to do it, when to do it, if you should do it, and on and on it goes. Sometimes you can't go to sleep until you work on the new idea.

THINKING TOO MUCH

Sometimes you can't get to sleep or stay asleep because you are thinking too much, often about the wrong thing. Your mind may be flooded with negative thoughts, or you may be rehearsing what happened, or what did not happen, or an embarrassing moment, etc. When you allow this kind of thinking to occur, you cannot relax because your emotions are involved and you are upset, angry, or fuming about something that happened. Know that these emotions stem out of fear--whether it is the fear of rejection or failure. Michael Pritchard once said, "fear is that little dark room where negatives are developed." Sometimes you can't sleep because you are spending a lot of time in the darkroom.

You may excessively worry about what others may be thinking about you. You might ponder the many different scenarios of a situation or even fume about something that has just happened, or something that happened years before.

HOW MUCH SLEEP DO YOU NEED?

Research on this topic has produced a range of suggested sleep time from 6.5 to 9 hours per night. Researchers pick a random sample of people to participate in their sleep study and therein is the problem. With a random sample there will be an unknown mixture of people with various temperament blends. Without understanding that the need for sleep is relative to a person's temperament blend, results will be skewed and even misleading. Those that routinely require the least amount of sleep (4 to 5 hours and sometimes less) to function well include the Choleric-Melancholy (D/C), the Choleric-Sanguine (D/I), and the Sanguine-Melancholy (I/C).

Those that require the most amount of sleep (eight or more) have Phlegmatic (S) as their primary temperament. When a person is Phlegmatic (S) first, they will fall asleep quickly and sleep through the night getting eight or more hours of sleep. When under stress this number will increase.

The other temperament blends vary as to the amount of sleep that is needed. The Melancholy-Phlegmatic (C/S) temperament usually requires around six hours of sleep. The Melancholy-Choleric (C/D) requires less than six hours of sleep. If a person is exhausted (regardless of their temperament blend) they will sleep beyond their normal need. Once well rested they will return to their normal sleep pattern.

No one knows how much sleep you need better than you. Remember, sleep is relative to your temperament blend. As a Sanguine-Melancholy you naturally fall into that four to six hour range of sleep needed in order to function well.

WHAT CAN YOU DO?

BE AWARE

Become aware of why you are not sleeping well. Consider the things mentioned in this chapter.

Become aware of how much sleep you need to feel good and have enough energy for the day. As a Sanguine-Melancholy, it is normal for you to function well on much less sleep than the reported averages.

TAKE CONTROL

Take control of your thoughts. Provide adequate alone time during the late evening or early morning to review the day and prepare for what you are going to do next.

When it is time to go to sleep, choose to not think about anything important or a problem that needs to be solved. Choose to think about those kind of things during your designated alone time. Choose to think about something that will not stir your emotions. Choose to think about something that is pleasant and relaxing and you will drift off to sleep.

19

SELF-AWARENESS EXERCISE

SELF-AWARENESS EXERCISE

To maximize your potential, become aware of how well you are in control in the areas listed below. Circle the number in each category that represents how you are doing on a scale of one to ten. Use the results of your self-awareness exercise to determine if there are areas in which you need to make adjustments.

I spend enough time with people	10	9	8	7	6	5	4	3	2	1
I spend adequate time alone	10	9	8	7	6	5	4	3	2	1
I have adequate coping skills	10	9	8	7	6	5	4	3	2	1
I control my thoughts and emotions	10	9	8	7	6	5	4	3	2	1
I control my moods	10	9	8	7	6	5	4	3	2	1
I am concerned about my image	10	9	8	7	6	5	4	3	2	1
I control my need to talk	10	9	8	7	6	5	4	3	2	1
I am being creative	10	9	8	7	6	5	4	3	2	1
I am a good self-coach	10	9	8	7	6	5	4	3	2	1
I use positive self-talk	10	9	8	7	6	5	4	3	2	1
I visualize success	10	9	8	7	6	5	4	3	2	1
I make healthy choices	10	9	8	7	6	5	4	3	2	1
I have a positive impact	10	9	8	7	6	5	4	3	2	1
I get enough sleep	10	9	8	7	6	5	4	3	2	1

Have your mate, a family member, or a significant person that knows you well rate the same categories on the scale of one to ten. Have discussions about the choices you both have made and compare. This will reveal the level of your self-awareness.

_____spends enough time with people	10 9 8 7 6 5 4 3 2 1
_____spends adequate time alone	10 9 8 7 6 5 4 3 2 1
_____has adequate coping skills	10 9 8 7 6 5 4 3 2 1
_____controls thoughts and emotions	10 9 8 7 6 5 4 3 2 1
_____controls their moods	10 9 8 7 6 5 4 3 2 1
_____is concerned about image	10 9 8 7 6 5 4 3 2 1
_____controls their need to talk	10 9 8 7 6 5 4 3 2 1
_____is being creative	10 9 8 7 6 5 4 3 2 1
_____is a good self-coach	10 9 8 7 6 5 4 3 2 1
_____uses positive self-talk	10 9 8 7 6 5 4 3 2 1
_____visualizes success	10 9 8 7 6 5 4 3 2 1
_____makes healthy choices	10 9 8 7 6 5 4 3 2 1
_____has a positive impact	10 9 8 7 6 5 4 3 2 1
_____gets enough sleep	10 9 8 7 6 5 4 3 2 1

20

THE USE OF MEDICATION

The efficacy of a drug does not prove that a particular mental disturbance is biochemically determined. For example, aspirin relieves headaches but no one contends that a headache is brought about by aspirin deficiency.

-COLIN ROSS & ALVIN PAM | MD & PH.D..

THE USE OF MEDICATION

I met with a twenty-one year old Sanguine-Melancholy that reported she was going crazy. A relationship had recently ended and she was not handling it very well. She explained that her thoughts were running wild and she was not able to sleep at night. She reached out for help trying to avoid taking medication to treat her anxiety and depression. Once I explained the natural temperament tendencies to her, she was able to relax, understanding that she was normal and not crazy. She followed through on my suggestions and she quickly pulled herself out of her depression and "crazy" feelings.

Those in the field of psychiatry, psychology, and counseling will tell you that a chemical disturbance in the brain causes issues like anxiety and depression as well as ADD, ADHD, and bipolar disorder. The use of medication for the treatment of these maladies needs to be addressed because they are some of the most common issues the Sanguine-Melancholy may face.

The most frequent recommendation one gets when seeking help from those in the medical and counseling professions, is to use medication. It is the common treatment choice--but is it correct? Is it possible to have a chemical imbalance in the brain that causes anxiety, depression, and bipolar disorder? A close examination may surprise you.

CHEMICAL IMBALANCE BLOOD TEST

I do not believe in the chemical imbalance theory because it cannot be proven with a blood test. Actually, no such blood test exists.

If you have ever been on one of these medications, you know this is true. You were not given a blood test to determine if your brain chemistry was out of balance, you were just given the medication based on the symptoms you shared with the doctor.

Doctors are scientists that operate on scientific facts to determine appropriate treatment for an ailment, but this is not true when it comes to issues such as anxiety, depression, being bipolar, and other diagnoses. Medication is assigned upon just hearing of the symptoms such as feeling blue or anxious, or an inability to sleep, or having emotional highs and lows.

Virtually all disorders that are said to be caused by a chemical-imbalance are determined only after hearing symptoms of the behavior without one piece of scientific evidence from the patient. Blood tests are given *after* medication is administered to determine the levels of the drugs ingested.

AN IRRESPONSIBLE DIAGNOSIS?

I went to my doctor years ago to get an explanation of an event that had occurred a few days earlier. I explained that I suddenly became confused and disoriented, I broke out in a cold sweat and my vision became blurry. I was unable to continue driving safely so I pulled into a parking lot. I thought my blood sugar had dropped and I needed some orange juice. Fortunately there was a grocery store near where I had parked. It took about twenty minutes before I could gain enough control to go into the store and get sugar into my system. It took about ten minutes of wandering around in the store (still a bit disoriented) before I finally found the orange juice. I drank it quickly and then paid the clerk. I slowly regained my senses and was able to continue on my journey.

After hearing my symptoms, my doctor of ten years looked at me and said, "I have some bad news for you, you have a tumor on your pancreas!" I was stunned! My first thought was *I have three months to live* and said, "Lord, I'm coming home." He then said he wanted a second opinion and walked out of the room to phone a colleague. At that moment my brother called. I told him the news and said I would call him back. I sat there lonely and numb. I had three months to live...who survives pancreatic cancer? I thought how my brother must be feeling as he waited on my return call. After what seemed like hours (actually about fifteen minutes) the doctor returned to the examination room. He said, "I lied, you have Hypoglycemia!"

My doctor, after hearing my symptoms, made a diagnosis. He did not suggest scanning for a tumor on my pancreas or giving me a glucose tolerance test. Was he irresponsible? Many would say that he was. Medical doctors are to gather sufficient scientific data before declaring a diagnosis—especially a potentially life-ending diagnosis.

What happened to me is an illustration of what happens every time someone is diagnosed with a so-called brain chemistry mental disorder. The diagnosis is given without any physical scientific data, only self-reported symptoms.

TWO DISSSENTING PSYCHIATRISTS

Dr. Collin Ross, a psychiatrist, was my supervisor for two years during my counseling internship. I asked him to discuss the correlation between low Serotonin and depression. It is believed by some that the depletion of serotonin, a brain chemical (neurotransmitter), is the cause of, or contributes to depression. His response to my question was immediate, "There is no correlation between low serotonin and depression." He explained that the research projects that had demonstrated a correlation were flawed in their methodology and the results were therefore unacceptable. For a detailed discussion, see *Pseudoscience In Biological Psychiatry, Blaming The Body* by Colin Ross, M. D. and Alvin Pam, Ph.D.

In regards to the use of medications for mental disorders, Dr. Ross states, "Despite vigorous laboratory investigation, no psychiatric disorder has thus far been cured by medication, not even manic disorder where lithium treatment has been so helpful. The efficacy of a drug does not prove that a particular mental disturbance is biochemically determined. For example, aspirin relieves headaches but no one contends that a headache is brought about by aspirin deficiency" (Ross & Pam, 1995).

Perhaps the strongest and most aggressive voice against biological psychiatry comes from Peter R. Breggin, M.D., a psychiatrist since the late 1960's. He says that psychiatric drugs have, "No specific therapeutic effect on any symptom or problems. Their main impact is to blunt and subdue the individual." He goes on to say, "Thus they [psychiatric drugs] produce a chemical lobotomy and a chemical straitjacket. Indeed, there is relatively little evidence that they are helpful to the patients themselves, while there is considerable evidence that psychosocial interventions are much better" (Breggin, 1994).

He does not stop there. In regards to antidepressants he states. "Since the antidepressants frequently make people feel worse, since they interfere with both psychotherapy and spontaneous improvement by blunting the emotions and confusing the mind, since most are easy tools for suicide, since they have many adverse physical side effects, since they can be difficult to withdraw from, and since there's little evidence for their effectiveness—it makes sense never to use them" (Breggin, 1994).

ANXIETY AND DEPRESSION

We are emotional beings. Individuals vary in the amount and intensity of emotion expressed based on their temperament blend, but everyone has emotions. This is stating the obvious but it needs to be said. The reason? Emotions fluctuate, sometimes widely due to an individual's positive or negative response to people and events.

As a therapist, I have dealt with many people who came to me because they were depressed. Depressing feelings are sometimes related to hormonal changes, like those experienced by women. I found a common theme in all my patients: they were thinking too much about the wrong thing. Before I go further please understand that some down feelings are not only appropriate but expected and normal. For example, if you were to lose a loved one to death it would be appropriate to feel depressed and have normal activities like eating, sleeping and working interrupted. After a period of time has elapsed, these functions return to normal and we continue our journey through life.

However, for the most part, those who report that they are depressed or anxious are stuck on a problem. Something has happened or something has not happened, someone did something to them or they did something to someone else...the list is endless. What I've noticed is that people are living examples of what Epictetus said 2,000 years ago, "Men are disturbed, not by things or events, but by the views (perceptions) which they take of them."

Depressed and anxious people disturb themselves by holding on to the view that is causing the disturbance. Depressed and anxious people are choosing their misery. People who frequently struggle with anxiety and depression are not trying to solve their problems, they are stuck in their problems. Depressed and anxious people lack coping skills and need to be taught how to identify options and be encouraged to choose one so they can move on in their journey through life.

The word "depressed" is a state of being, so it is more accurate to say "depressing" which represents an action. One who is "depressing" is holding something down continually. Once that something is let go, then they are no longer "depressing."

Being depressed or anxious is therefore not a brain chemistry problem rather it is a "thinking" problem that needs to be corrected. Once corrected, the depressing feelings leave.

Philippians 4:6-7 states, "Do not be anxious about anything, but in every situation, by prayer and petition, with thanksgiving, present your requests to God. And the peace of God, which transcends all understanding, will guard your hearts and your minds in Christ Jesus."

BIPOLAR DISORDER

People who are labeled bipolar have a natural temperament blend (Sanguine -Melancholy) that when not controlled, will show noticeable and sometimes sudden changes in their normal mood state. The two tendencies are not only opposite, they are oppositional to each other. For example, the social side needs to be with people and the analytical side needs to be alone.

When the individual does not control these tendencies, they will have changes in their normal mood state. They do not have a chemical-imbalance issue, they have a self-control issue.

WHAT IF MEDICATIONS HELP?

When discussing this issue with patients that are on medication I have been asked how do I explain that the medication helped them get better?

TRANQUILIZERS

I have mentioned that I worked in a mental hospital where we were required to give each patient a list of the medications that were being used—one or more of which would be administered to them. This list included all of the current popular medications on the market. The list was called "Tranquilizers." A tranquilizer is a calming drug that will blunt the emotions from being expressed. The truth is that if you give a "tranquilizer" to one who is emotional, anxious, or upset of course they will calm down. This is why I have said that *medication will do for you what you will not do for yourself.* You can calm yourself, or take a drug to calm you.

Part of being human is possessing the capability of controlling your emotions. Some choose to and others do not. If you are depressed for an extended period of time, you can choose to stop. If you are upset for an extended period of time, you can choose not to be. If you are being emotional for an extended period of time, you can choose not to. You take a pill, you feel better—the medication did for you what you chose not to do for yourself! Now granted, some upsetting events make it more difficult to calm yourself—a traumatic event often requires more time to adjust. Lots of people routinely get upset over little things and are anxious and emotional. Sometimes emotions fluctuate widely and sometimes people choose to hang on to what is disturbing them for the rest of their life. These people depend on medication to keep them level when they could do it themselves by applying coping skills.

PLACEBO EFFECT

We cannot rule out the placebo effect which means that one has a positive response just because they took a pill thinking it would help. Most everyone has heard of an experiment that has been conducted whereby a "sugar pill" was given to someone to see if they reported a positive response believing that it was medication.

THE EFFICACY OF A DRUG

Remember Dr. Ross' comment, "The efficacy of a drug does not prove that a particular mental disturbance is biochemically determined. For example, aspirin relieves headaches but no one contends that a headache is brought about by aspirin deficiency" (Ross & Pam, 1995).

SUMMARY

The chemical-imbalance theory is presented as fact by medical doctors, psychiatrists, therapists, and the media despite a complete lack of scientific data. No lab tests have been developed to determine the level of neurotransmitters in the brain to support a "mental illness" diagnosis. This is the major theme of those who are opposed to this theory. Furthermore, a "balance" of neurotransmitters has not been established in order to measure it against a so-called "imbalance."

I know of nothing that is more irresponsible in the field of medicine than the chemical-imbalance theory. Dr. Peter Breggin and David Cohen in, *Your Drug May Be Your Problem: How and Why To Stop Taking Psychiatric Medications* (1999), claims that "biochemical imbalances are the only diseases spread by word of mouth."

We easily lose sight of the basic truth that human beings think, feel and make choices. No one can make another person angry, sad or happy without their permission. We are born selfish creatures and seek what is best for "me." We want what we want and we want it now. When we cannot get what we want, we choose to disturb ourselves, sometimes to the point that we get labeled with a diagnosis.

Epictetus had it figured out nearly 2,000 years ago when he said that we are disturbed not by what happens to us but by the views we take about what happens to us. Dr. Glasser is equally clear when he said that we choose the misery we experience. Victor Frankl said while he was in a concentration camp during WWII that everything could be taken away from him but his right to choose the attitude about what is happening to him. People make choices.

The chemical-imbalance theory neither relieves, reduces, or diverts the accountability and responsibility of the individual for the choices they make. However, the chemical imbalance position makes it easy for an individual to blame something or someone else for their behavior; "I am this way because my mother, father, brother, sister, aunt, uncle, friend, neighbor, dog or cat did this or that to me!" **The age in which we live encourages blaming everything and everyone else for one's bad behavior but the one behaving badly.**

If you are a Sanguine-Melancholy and your behavior is causing you some difficulty in some of the areas mentioned in this book, remember you have a marvelous temperament that is capable of great achievements and creativity. Your degree of success in life is directly related to your willingness to control your emotions, conquer your fears, and develop healthy coping skills.

21

SUCCESS STORIES

SUCCESS STORIES

"I do not want to ever have that feeling again!"

"Now that you point it out, I see it."

"I realized that I was the problem and that gave me great hope. I could fix me but I cannot fix others."

These quotes mentioned above are from Sanguine-Melancholies that have made changes. They illustrate the heart attitude that is needed not just by Sanguine-Melancholies but by everyone. I am going to give you a glimpse into the hearts and minds of people that I have had the privilege to know. Each one of them has struggled with some of the issues mentioned in this book, battled against their natural weaknesses and won.

SHE MADE A DECISION

It is difficult for a Sanguine-Melancholy to control their emotions once embarrassed, but Bridget did. She is the 16 year old with fantastic writing ability. Although she is 16, at times she has demonstrated a maturity level that exceeds many adults I've known.

Once she had made a decision that she later deeply regretted because the results she expected did not happen and she was deeply embarrassed. Rather than reacting with extreme emotion, she decided instead to just learn from that decision. In reviewing her decision she said to me, "I am not going to do that again because I do not want to ever have that feeling again!" She was able to use her emotions to fuel better decision-making rather than dwelling on the past and her mistakes.

ADAPT THIS PERSPECTIVE

A friend of mine, who is Sanguine-Melancholy, is successful, accountable, responsible, and a great father and husband. After reading this book he said that his thinking had changed. He had thought that everybody else was the problem in his life but after reading the book he said, "I realized that I was the problem and that gave me great hope. I could fix me but I cannot fix others."

Whatever problems he was referring to are minor because he is living his life consciously, with principles and purpose. He has a strong Christian faith that he demonstrates in his life daily. He is devoted to his wife and children and is a great example of what can be accomplished when one is accountable, willing to change and focused on a purpose greater than self. Anyone who follows his example is destined to have a meaningful and satisfying life.

GAINED INSIGHT

She and her husband were having difficulties communicating. To make a point, she would often elevate her emotions and become a bit aggressive. To avoid conflict he would retreat to the back of his man cave. During a counseling session she did what she had been doing for years...her emotions were elevated to drive home her point. He responded as he had done for years and shut down. After a few minutes had passed, I pointed out to her what had just happened. It took a few minutes for her to process the event and then said, "Now that you point it out, I see it." Her response revealed her heart because she made a decision that is typically difficult for a Sanguine-Melancholy to make--especially when told they are wrong. She was not aware of how she had responded to her husband. Once it was made clear to her, she decided to change how she communicated to her husband.

HE TURNED IT AROUND

A friend of mine called me on a Saturday because he was deeply concerned about his friend Jim. Jim was in his 40's and had made a mess of his life. He had a sales job but was not selling. His wife, who supported the family financially, told him that she was no longer going to tolerate his lack of earning money. An argument erupted and he left to go to a bar. A few too many drinks and an attempt to drive himself home resulted in a DWI.

His wife was at a breaking point and so was his boss. Jim was good at finding prospects but he was not good at making a sale. His last sale was six months before and his boss was about to terminate his employment. Out of desperation his friend called me. I was asked to speak to Jim about his Sanguine-Melancholy temperament and offer some insight and direction.

The phone conversation lasted about an hour and a half. I explained his temperament tendencies and how he had lived his life based on fear. Jim was afraid of being rejected, being embarrassed, and failing. I explained that his image was more important than his wife and children and that he was being selfish and self-centered. I encouraged Jim to make a decision to face his fear and decide to ask his prospects for the order.

Jim commented that the things I had told him were not only close to being right, they had "hit the nail on the head." Jim took ownership of what he had heard and made a decision to ask for the order regardless of his fear. I encouraged him not to tell his wife but to just go do it the next week.

I received a call late Tuesday afternoon from my friend to report what Jim had been doing for the first two days of the week. He started asking for the sale from his prospects and in two days he had made four sales. With this renewed success, his behavior towards his wife also shifted which caused her to also shift. Because he made a decision to overcome his fear of looking bad, his career and his marriage improved.

AT AGE 13

Kaleb, at age thirteen read the manuscript of this book. Here are his comments:

> I took away from the book that the Sanguine-Melancholy can be very moody and selfish. Their moodiness can affect their whole life and others. At the end of the book I thought that this book was like a mirror; it's a reflection of myself. This book helped me know how to keep control of my emotions and to look deeper in myself. I learned how to put God and others first instead of myself and not be selfish."

LONG TERM DECISION

I saw Linda for several sessions many years ago. I explained her natural tendencies as a Sanguine-Melancholy and that she was giving in to her natural weaknesses. She was having difficulty controlling her emotions and had turned to alcohol and drugs to bury her pain. Many relationships had been destroyed because of her irresponsible and out-of-control behavior. She seemed to get it but I wasn't sure if she would follow through with the direction I had offered.

Years passed when I had a chance meeting with Linda. My wife and I were eating at a restaurant when a family got up to leave and was passing our table. Linda stopped and said, "Do you remember me?" She said that she wanted me to know that the information that I shared with her had changed her life. She learned to control her emotions, thoughts and stopped being sensitive to how people responded to her. She had settled down, married, and was enjoying a fulfilling life. She had followed through!

IT TAKES ONE TO KNOW ONE

I have known Joyce for several years. When we first met, her son was around two years of age. He was now four and showing signs of disruptive behavior in kindergarten but not at home. She came to see me to get some tweaking on understanding her temperament because her son was also a Sanguine-Melancholy. She was hoping that as she learned more about their temperament, she could better help her son.

One of her biggest takeaways of the conversation and having the same temperament as her son was that she understood that he took her "no" responses as rejection. She now explains to him why she says "no" so that he doesn't associate her "no's" to him as rejection.

I THOUGHT I WAS GOING CRAZY

Nichole is a twenty-two year old attractive Sanguine-Melancholy that came to me saying that she thought she was going crazy. Her thoughts were running wild, she had just been rejected by her boyfriend, and she was not sleeping well. She was beginning to feel depressed so she reached out for help.

I explained her natural temperament tendencies as a Sanguine-Melancholy. She was so relieved just knowing where all of her emotions were coming from and that she was not going crazy. I explained some things she could do to address her temperament tendencies and she followed through. The next time I saw her she explained how she was able to gain control over her thoughts and emotions so they were not controlling her. I have rarely seen anyone embrace the reality of their temperament tendencies so quickly and take steps to control the negatives.

NEVER GIVE UP

Dr. Gary Fusco is a therapist in Florida and has been trained in the use of the temperament model of behavior in counseling. The following story is one of many he has shared with me over the years. Ellen's story illustrates what can happen when you are determined to get beyond the issues that prevent you from maximizing your potential. Here is Ellen's story as reported by Dr. Gary Fusco:

Ellen had a long history of battling Bulimia, alcohol, and drugs, and had been diagnosed with Bipolar disorder when she was fifteen. She had been involved in hundreds of relationships, most of them sexual and most of them one-night-stands. She was experiencing extreme nervous behavior, anxiety, and depression. She had been seeing counselors and psychiatrists for seventeen years who did nothing to improve her condition except to give her medications. I was the 18th counselor she came to because she was still in desperate need of help. I was the first one to approach her life struggles by explaining her natural temperament tendencies. When given the temperament assessment, Ellen scored clearly as a Sanguine-Melancholy and was demonstrating many of the out of control tendencies of her temperament blend. Because of her opposing and opposite temperaments, Ellen experienced sudden and dramatic changes in her behavior which convinced the previous 17 counselors that she was bipolar.

The internal tension that she suffered from would come to a head every weekend. When I asked her to describe an average week to me I learned that she was allowing her Sanguine side to completely dominate from Monday morning to Friday evening. She would begin like a shot Monday morning at 6 AM working two jobs during the day, and then she would play and be busy with her crafts and other activities until late each evening. All of this at a non-stop, intense pace with very little sleep. Come Friday evening she would crash and become a complete recluse all weekend. Almost paralyzed, she would see no one and just sleep and feel depressed. Having been pushed to the max, her Melancholy side was screaming out, "OK, that's it! I have had enough and I cannot take this anymore! We are checking out for some overdue alone time and for some much needed rest." Then Monday morning the cycle would start all over again.

To change her behavior, each temperament need had to be met and a sense of balance had to be restored. I told her she had to work less hours each day and when she came home she had to rest, wind down, and have some quiet time. On the weekends she could pull out her arts and crafts and have a ball. Ellen followed-through with my suggestions and quickly started to feel relaxed and less anxious.

Her moods stabilized and she began to get the sleep she needed. Ellen was now in control of her temperament tendencies that she had allowed to control her behavior. In just four weeks time she was able to wean herself off of her four medications, quit drinking, and even quit smoking! Learning to control her Sanguine/Melancholy tendencies enabled her to bring balance to her life.

SUMMARY

These stories are real and they represent what can happen when you make a decision to control your natural tendencies.

CONCLUSION

When the Sanguine-Melancholy exercises self-control and is focused and committed to a goal bigger than themselves, they outperform everyone else. These are talented, capable, and creative people.

DAVID'S EXAMPLE

One of the greatest men in history is King David (1040–970 BC). He wrote literature that has encouraged countless millions for three thousand years. But great as David was, he still had his struggles. Reading the material he wrote shows us that he had deep passions and at times paralyzing fears. Still it was said of him (and only him) that there goes a man after God's own heart!

It's been said of King David that when he was bad, he was very bad, but when he was good, he was very good. David's life demonstrates the ups and downs of having the Sanguine-Melancholy temperament. He struggled but he also overcame his struggles to accomplish great things.

Like King David, people with the Sanguine-Melancholy temperament have made enormous contributions for centuries. The artists, writers, poets, and the greatest actors and actresses are almost always Sanguine-Melancholy. They have such natural ability that Hollywood is full of these talented and creative people. They write our songs, sing our songs, write poetry, dance, paint, draw, decorate, etc. Name a creative expression and this person will likely be the one doing it the best of all.

LASTING IMPACTS

When a Sanguine-Melancholy manages to control their fears and their reactions to unfavorable situations, they can leave a lasting impact on the people in their lives. Some of the finest and most successful people I know fit this category. One is a businessman I've known for fifteen years. He is hard working, insightful, and full of character. I count him a dear friend. Another friend I've known for four years is also gifted, stable, and a man of honor. I am a better person for knowing him. I have benefited from all of these relationships.

My wife has become dear friends with a wonderful lady who is Sanguine-Melancholy. This lady is a fine person, known by many and loved by everyone. Once while teaching a group, I casually mentioned her name and someone in the group abruptly spoke up and said, "I know her!" She makes friends everywhere she goes and it is almost impossible to forget an encounter with her because she is so winsome and engaging. If you live in the Dallas, Texas area you've probably met her too!

IT DOESN'T END HERE.

The value of reading this book does not lie in the knowledge that you now have about your temperament--the value lies in the application. Knowing what to do and doing it are two entirely different things. James 1:22 states, *"But be doers of the word and not hearers only, deceiving yourselves."* This is teaching us that if you know what to do and you're not doing it, then you are deceived. The deception is believing that knowing is sufficient. It is not. You and I must do what we know is right.

It is possible to know all the right things, to have wisdom and insight and teach others, and yet still follow a course of extreme foolishness! Our choices will always determine the quality of our life. Charles Swindoll said, "Wisdom occurs when knowledge produces obedience."

Do not let what you read just be added knowledge, make the choice to let it change your life.

A NOTE FROM THE AUTHOR

I mentioned in the introduction that my long journey began in 1974 to understand and develop the temperament model of behavior. I did not know what I was looking for, I was just looking because I was so fascinated with the concept of temperament.

The greatest and most rewarding discovery I made is what this book is about. I found that the greatest potential, the most naturally gifted, and the most creative temperament is the Sanguine-Melancholy.

I discovered the good, the bad, and the ugly side of this temperament blend. I have seen many achieve great success and do wonderful creative things with their natural abilities. I have also seen many fail to maximize their potential mainly because of giving in to their fears and not having self-control.

It is my deep desire that if you are struggling with your journey through this life that the pages of this book will help you see the creative potential that you possess as a Sanguine-Melancholy (I-C).

To maximize your potential, to be productive, and to be at peace, take accountability for your behavior, be responsible for your choices, control your natural tendencies, and express your creativity. Overcome your fears so they do not paralyze who you want to become. Take control of your thoughts and emotions so they do not control you. If you want to maximize the potential of the temperament gift that you have been given, identify the areas that give you difficulty and develop effective coping skills.

Always remember, the choices you make turn around and make you. Live well, make good choices and you will maximize your potential.

May God bless you in your
journey through this life.

John T. Cocoris

ABOUT THE AUTHOR

John T. Cocoris has devoted his life since the early 1970's to developing the temperament model of behavior. John has a B.A. from Tennessee Temple University, a Masters of Theology (Th. M.) from Dallas Theological Seminary, a Masters in Counseling (M.A.) from Amberton University, and a Doctorate in Psychology (Psy. D.) from California Coast University. John is a licensed counselor in the state of Texas.

John established Profile Dynamics in the early 1980's to develop and promote the temperament model of behavior for use in business and counseling. He has been a management consultant since 1984 and has worked with a variety of companies giving seminars for training managers and sales people. John has been interviewed on the radio and has been featured numerous times on COPE, a national cable TV talk show.

John has written many books and manuals about the temperament model including: The Temperament Model of Behavior, Understanding Your Natural Tendencies; The Creative Temperament, The Sanguine-Melancholy (I/C); 7 Steps To A Better You, How To Develop Your Natural Tendencies; Discover Your Child's Temperament, Born With Natural Tendencies; The Problem Person in You Life, Understanding People of Extremes; A Therapist's Guide to The Temperament Model of Behavior; How to Supervise Others Using The Temperament Model of Behavior; Effective Selling Using The Temperament Model of Behavior; The DISC II Temperament Assessment; The DISC II Temperament Assessment User Guide; DISC II Library, 15 Pattern Series; The DISC 3 Temperament Assessment; The DISC 3 Temperament Assessment User Guide.

APPENDIX

HOW TO DEAL WITH FRUSTRATION

As a Sanguine-Melancholy, remember that you have an enormous depth of emotion because of your temperament blend. This is both good news and bad news. The good news is that you bring a great deal of passion to whatever you do in life. You have the ability to feel every emotion deeply. The bad news is that this depth of emotion is also at times, difficult to control and manage

Without a plan to deal with frustration, you will continue to be surprised, overwhelmed, and lose emotional control. To break out of this cycle of moving from one emotional moment to the next, you need something in place to stop you from reacting emotionally. The following system called How To Deal With Frustration will do that.

I call this system a "mental safety net." Using this system will prevent an immediate, inappropriate reaction and will help you avoid being derailed emotionally. If you practice this you will gain control over your emotions, fears, and anxieties allowing you to respond appropriately to difficult and frustrating moments. Here's how it works:

A. FRUSTRATION COMES FROM EXPECTATIONS NOT BEING MET
Once frustrated you allow emotions to be expressed.

B. FRUSTRATION MAY BE DIVIDED INTO TWO CATEGORIES:
1. You expect people to perform a certain way to meet your standards.
2. You expect events to turn out exactly the way you desire.

The truth is that sometimes your expectations for people and events are unrealistic and sometimes you place too much importance on your expectations. If people do not perform the way you expect, or events do not turn out the way you anticipated, you get disappointed, frustrated, even angry. Sometimes you get depressed or have self-destructive thoughts. The idea is to STOP the thinking process that leads to an emotional reaction by thinking of the word ADJUST. Then do one or more of the following four things to adjust.

1. CHOOSE TO NOT GET FRUSTRATED
Everything is a choice.

2. CHANGE YOUR PERCEPTION
Look for a different/positive interpretation
It's not the event that's important; it's the interpretation of the event

Ask yourself: "How can I look at this so it's not a problem?"

3. ACKNOWLEDGE WHAT **IS** WITHOUT MAKING A VALUE JUDGMENT
Be objective and always operate on facts.

A person's opinion of himself seriously biases his interpretation of what is happening.

4. DO NOT TAKE IT PERSONALLY
Have compassion

To help you remember these four ways to adjust, write ADJUST on a 3x5 card in bold letters. On the reverse side of the card, write out the four ways to adjust. Make up several of these and place them in obvious places so that you will never be without one (wallet, car, briefcase, purse, etc.).

This card will remind you to ADJUST and to not react emotionally. We all need to be told once and reminded often. Carry the card with you everywhere you go. At the slightest hint of frustration pull out the card and read it. If you choose to act on one of the four it will prevent an emotional reaction.

DEVELOP A PHILOSOPHY OF LIFE

Having a Philosophy of Life represents a long term and more permanent solution to building a lifestyle way of dealing with life experiences. A Philosophy of Life is simply deciding on the rules, regulations, and principles upon which you are going to live your life. A Philosophy of Life is how you are going to conduct yourself.

Using the ADJUST approach is actually the beginning stage of developing your Philosophy of Life. Having your response clearly written down enables you to be prepared for disappointments, embarrassments, etc. As you practice it to deal with life, you will develop a lifestyle way of thinking. Eventually you will not react to frustrating moments in a negative way, you will respond with healthy, appropriate behavior.

Below is a partial list of statements that I've collected over the years. Recall one of more of these when life throws you a curve. It will enable you to focus, not on the problem, but on the solution. By recalling one or more of these statements, your thoughts are redirected from negative to positive and you will be well on your way to developing emotional control.

Use the list to get started, and make time to develop your own. Have as a goal for the rest of your life to collect pithy statements that reflect wisdom and give guidance. Imagine how different your life would be if you were on a mission to find what others have learned about how to handle life's struggles.

Your purpose is to collect and *practice*--not just collect. If you do this, you would have less time to think about problems and disappointments because you will be too busy thinking about solutions. As you develop your own list, write them on a 3x5 card and keep them with you so you can look at them several times a day. Continue doing this until the saying is easily recalled from memory. At the appropriate time, recall one or more of the sayings or one-liners to redirect your thinking and control your emotions.

1. Silence is sometimes the best response.

2. When you lose, don't lose the lesson.

3. Remember that not getting what you want is sometimes a wonderful stroke of luck.

4. He who is good at making excuses is seldom good for anything else.

5. Don't let a little dispute destroy a relationship.

6. Kindness is difficult to give away because it keeps coming back.

7. Nothing ruins the truth like stretching it.

8. You can tell how big a person is by what it takes to discourage him.

9. He who angers you controls you.

10. Don't sweat the small stuff; everything is small stuff.

11. You cannot reason with an unreasonable person so do not try.

12. Never argue.

CHANGE IS AN INSIDE JOB!

REFERENCES

Breggin, P. R. (1994). *Toxic psychiatry: Why therapy, empathy and love must replace the drugs, electroshock, and biochemical theories of the "new psychiatry".* New York, NY: St. Martin's Press.

Breggin, P. R., & Cohen, D. (1999). *Your drug may be your problem: How and why to stop taking psychiatric medications.* Philadelphia, PA: Da Capo Press.

Buss, A. H., & Robert P. (1975). *A temperament theory of personality development.* New York, NY: John Wiley & Sons.

Chess, S., & Alexander, T. (1987). *Know your child.* New York, NY: BasicBooks, Inc., Publishers.

Clapperboard designed by Javier Calvo Patiño from the thenounproject.com

Compassion designed by Scott Lewis from the thenounproject.com

Dobson, J. C. (1987). *Parenting isn't for cowards: Dealing confidently with the frustrations of child-rearing.* Waco, TX: Word Books.

Eysenck, H. J. (1967). *The biological basis of personality.* Springfield, IL: Bannerstone House.

Eysenck, H. J. (1953). *The structure of human personality.* London: Methuen & Co. LTD.

Eysenck, H. J., & Eysenck, M. W. (1985). *Personality and individual differences.* New York, NY : Plenum Press.

Eysenck, H. J., & Eysenck, S. B. G. (1969). *Personality structure and measurement.* San Diego, CA: Robert R. Knapp, Publisher.

Galen. (1968). *Galen's system of physiology and medicine*. (R.E. Siegel, Trans.). New York, NY: S. Karger.

Glasser, W. (1999). *Choice theory: A new psychology of personal freedom*. New York, NY: Harper Perennial.

Gray, M. C. (2001, June 29). Pyscho-Cybernetics [Review of the book *Psycho-cybernetics*]. Retrieved from http://www.profitadvisors.com/psychoc.shtml

Hallesby, O. (1962). *Temperament & the christian faith*. Minneapolis, MN: Augsburg Publishing House.

Hippocrates. (1937). T*he genuine works of Hippocrates*. (F, Adams, Trans.). Baltimore, MD: The Williams & Wilkins Company. (Original work published 1939).

Kant, I. (1974). *Anthropology from a pragmatic point of view*. (M. J. Gregor, Trans.). The Hague, Netherlands: Martinus Nijhoff. (Original work published 1798).

Keirsey, D., & Bates, M. (1984). *Please understand me: Character & temperament types*. Del Mar, CA: Prometeus Nemesis Book Company.

LaHaye, T. F. (1967). *Spirit controlled temperament*. Whaton: Tyndale House Publishers.

LaHaye, T. F. (1977). *Understanding the male temperament*. Old Tappan, NJ: Fleming H. Revell Co.

LaHaye, T. F. (1984). *Your temperament: Discover its potential*. Wheaton, IL: Tyndale House Publishers.

LaHaye, T. F. (1971). *Transformed temperaments*. Wheaton, IL: Tyndale House Publishers.

Maltz, M. (1960). *Psycho-cybernetics*. Englewood Cliffs, NJ: Prentice-Hall, Inc.

Marston, W. M. (1979). *Emotions of normal people*. Minneapolis, MN: Persona Press, Inc.

Merrill, D. W., & Reid, R.H. (1981) *Personal styles & effective performance.* Bradner, PA: Chilton Book Company.

National Institute of Mental Health. (2014) Causes. *National Institute of Mental Health.* Retrieved from http://www.nimh.nih.gov/health/topics/depression/index.shtml#part2

National Institute of Mental Health. (2014) Signs and symptoms. *National Institute of Mental Health.* Retrieved from http://www.nimh.nih.gov/health/topics/depression/index.shtml#part2

Nordqvist, C. (2014). Signs and symptoms. *Medical News Today.* Retrieved from http://www.medicalnewstoday.com/articles/8933.php#signs_and_symptoms

Ross, C., & Pam, A. (1995). *Pseudoscience in biological psychiatry: Blaming the body.* New York, NY: John Wiley & Sons, Inc.